LULWORTH ENCYCLOPAEDIA

Covering the **Lulworth Ranges** and the Dorset coastal parishes of **West Lulworth**, **East Lulworth**, **Tyneham**, **Steeple**, **East Holme** and **Coombe Keynes**.

Rodney Legg

DORSET PUBLISHING COMPANY
at the WINCANTON PRESS NATIONAL SCHOOL
NORTH STREET WINCANTON SOMERSET BA9 9AT

For **Nathaniel Oakes-Ash**
after his Flower's Barrow walk

Public access is described as it was the time the book was researched. All and any opportunities to enter the Lulworth Ranges are subject to strict limitations on the ground and apply only as permitted by the Royal Armoured Corps. Elsewhere, paths are also liable to changes — from both natural causes and legal diversion. Any obstructions or other difficulties should be reported to the local highway authority. Contact the Rights of Way Office, Transportation and Engineering Department, County Hall, Dorchester, Dorset DT1 1XJ (01-305-251-000)

Publishing details
First published 1998.
Published by Dorset Publishing Company at the Wincanton Press, National School, North Street, Wincanton, Somerset BA9 9AT (01-963-325-83) to whom updatings may be sent, addressed to the author. Distribution by Halsgrove, Lower Moor Way, Tiverton, Devon EX16 6SS (01-884-243-242).

Printing credits
Typeset by Reg Ward. Printed in Somerset by F. W. B. Printing, Bennetts Mead, Southgate Road, Wincanton, Somerset BA9 9EB (01-963-337-55).

International standard book number
ISBN 0 948699 47 7

Rodney Legg, with 50 books to his name, has emerged as Dorset's premier historian of the twentieth century. In 1968 he founded *Dorset County Magazine* and went on to edit 114 issues. Other publications followed. His current title is *Dorset Country Magazine.*

Legg was born in 1947, at Easter Road, in the Bournemouth suburb of Moordown. As well as countryside topics he has specialised in military history, producing standard works such as *Dorset at War, D-Day Dorset,* and *Battle of Britain Dorset.*

In the archaeological field he managed a belated first with the transcription and printing, in collaboration with Lyme Regis author John Fowles, of John Aubrey's *Monumenta Britannica.* This pioneering magnum opus of antiquarian fieldwork had lain unpublished in the Bodleian Library at Oxford for three centuries. *Romans in Britain* followed, and a study of the *Stonehenge Antiquaries,* then *Stanton Drew: Great Western Temple.*

He is particularly proud to have devised, tramped, photographed and published a total of more than 500 circular country walks that cover three thousand miles of rights of way in Dorset and Somerset.

All the while he has been in the thick of environmental battles. Having been the founder of Tyneham Action Group and its successor organisations – a role documented by Patrick Wright in his book *The Village that Died for England* – he saw success of a sort with the Defence Ministry creating public access opportunities at Lulworth on a scale unprecedented for military firing ranges.

Nationally, he is at the forefront of the countryside movement, being chairman of the Open Spaces Society and a member of the governing council of the National Trust.

His escape from all this is to warden Steep Holm island, in the Bristol Channel, as a nature reserve memorial to his friend Kenneth Allsop, the broadcaster from Powerstock.

A to Z
self-indexing entries

Durdle Door: 'The Arched Rock near West Lulworth,' as this print was captioned

Alms Grove – known locally as Ameswood; a small wood on the south shoulder of the Purbeck Hills where the gated road branches down to Tyneham (SY 895 816). It is now inside the Lulworth Ranges but was formerly common land, hence the "Alms" element, so its local name may be a case of a silent "l". On the other hand it might originally have been Haime's Grove. The hames were curved bars fitted with loops and used to fasten the trace to the collar of a horse. It was pronounced "ames" in Dorset, as was the name of Haime, a family frequently recorded in East Lulworth parish registers from 1758 onwards.

Arish Mell – this dramatic gap in the chalk cliffs of Worbarrow Bay (SY 885 803) inside the Lulworth Ranges is passed by the main coastal range path, when it is available for use, but no access is allowed to the sea. Cows used to come down on to the beach. The first blockages were with dragon teeth anti-tank defences and obsolete stationary tanks as pillboxes in 1940. Then it became fully absorbed into the Lulworth Tank Ranges [1943] and was chosen for the outfall of the waste water-pipe from the Atomic Energy Establishment, Winfrith, which was laid directly into the sea [1957] as a precaution in case of radioactive discharges.

The first "mill of *Lulleworth*" may have been here [1234] and would have had to be tidal, like that at Christchurch, rather than relying on fresh-water power. "Mell" was rendered "Mill" throughout the Middle Ages, not that any traces of it remain, and the purest form of this now beautiful name is "Arse Mill" – as a topographical reference to its appearance as a slit between the smooth buttocks of the chalk hills.

The lost road inland from Arish Mell to White Lodge at East Lulworth is now within the barbed wire of the ranges. It passed Sea Vale Farm, then the site of New Barn, and skirted chalkpits on the edge of the appropriately named Old Marl Plantation.

Baltington – locally known as Backington, inside the Lulworth Ranges on the northern side of the valley between Tyneham and Worbarrow (SY 876 804). The name was recorded as Baltingeton in 1287. Its meaning is unknown. I tentatively suggest there may have been an earlier form of Baecington, "farm of the ridge dwellers", which would accurately describe its situation immediately beneath Whiteway Hill and the hill-fort of Flower's Barrow.

Baring – wealthy **William Baring** MP [died 19 July 1820], fourth son of the eminent financier Sir Francis Baring [1740-1810], drowned at Lulworth and has a memorial in East Lulworth parish church.

Battle of Britain – the Dorset coast was the frontline throughout the Luftwaffe offensive of the long, hot summer of 1940. The sound of the Merlin engines of the defending Spitfires and the sight of their vapour trails were everyday experience and offshore Junkers Ju87 "Stuka" dive-bombers closed the English Channel to allied shipping. Soon the action started to fall out of the sky.

The crash in Tyneham parish, on Povington Heath, of Messerschmitt Bf110 fighter-bomber 2N+EP, in a forced-landing, brought the first two German flyers to be taken prisoner in the Battle of Britain [11 July 1940]. They were Oberleutnant Gerhard Kadow, pilot [see his entry], and Gefreiter Helmut Scholz, gunner, of the 9th Staffel Zerstörergeschwader 76, from Laval. The kill was claimed by Spitfires of 609 Squadron from RAF Warmwell, near Dorchester.

A Hurricane of 213 Squadron from RAF Exeter crash-landed on the "C" Range, Lulworth Camp, after engaging German aircraft [11 August 1940]. Sergeant Pilot Snowdon was unhurt and his fighter repairable.

Messerschmitt Bf110 3M+KH belonging to the 1st Staffel of II Gruppe, Zerstörergeschwader 2 crashed at

Priory Farm, East Holme, on one of Dorset's busiest days during the air war [25 August 1940]. The stricken aircraft crashed to ground about a thousand yards from the sea.

Equally unfortunate that day were the crew of another Bf110, almost certainly Hans Carschel and Unteroffizier Klose in 3U+BD of Zerstörergeschwader 26, who crashed at Egliston, between Tyneham and Kimmeridge. Their Geschwader was named Horst Wessel after the Nazi subject of a militant anti-semitic song which became a national anthem.

Minutes later a third Bf110 (3U+DS), also belonging to Geschwader Horst Wessel, crash-landed near Gaulter Gap, beside Kimmeridge Bay. Crewmen Fritz Schupp and Karl Nechwatal were taken prisoner. Their aircraft carried three “kill” bars, denoting victories over RAF planes.

Both these Bf110s were claimed by Spitfires from Warmwell. The German aircraft had been taking part in an abortive raid on the Parnell Aircraft Company at Yate, near Chipping Sodbury.

Another Bf110, also apparently belonging to Zerstörergeschwader 26 and involved in the attack on the Westland Aircraft factory at Yeovil — where a hundred civilians were killed in a direct hit on an air-raid shelter — crashed into the sea 2,000 yards off the Arish Mell Gap [7 October 1940]. It was claimed by Spitfires of 609 Squadron from Warmwell.

Battle Plain — on the north-east edge of the Lulworth Ranges, half a mile south of Holme Lane, westwards from Army red flag no. 59 (SY 908 847). Mainly of interest for its name, which is said to commemorate a Civil War skirmish. The area is largely covered by post-war pine plantations and even on the civilian side of the military fence there is no public access.

Belhuish Valley — delightful chalkland combe, a mile north of West Lulworth, into which runs a no-through road from the B3071 to Belhuish Farm (SY 829 830). The farmhouse and barn are substantially seventeenth and eighteen century in date with later additions.

Walkers can explore further on West Lulworth public footpath 3 which continues southwards beside Belhuish Coppice, and links with path number 2 to return to the village. Downland on the western slopes of Belhuish Valley was part of the mediaeval Lulworth Common.

The spot where the little lane drops down from the main road is known locally as the Old Hill (SY 835 832). Belhuish Farmhouse is the home of thatcher Rod Miller; hence the mountain of reed stacked nearby.

Bindon Abbey – the Cistercian Abbey of Bindon was founded below Bindon Hill, to the east of Lulworth Cove [circa 1150] but soon moved to a different site, inland near Wool [1172] and took with it the name Bindon Abbey. Its seaside location was north-east of Little Bindon (SY 831 798), in a sheltered vale. (See Little Bindon entry for more details.)

Black Hawk – United States steam-freighter, sunk in Worbarrow Bay by a torpedo from a German U-boat [29 December 1944]. Her stern was blown to pieces and the crew scrambled to safety after beaching her bows.

Blackmanston Farm – south-east of Steeple village, a kilometre east of the Lulworth Ranges (SY 915 807), this cluster of buildings is typical in showing the continuity of habitation in Purbeck. The present farm incorporates a two-up, two-down dwelling of the sixteenth century that was extended in the seventeenth century and later.

As with most of the small scattered settlements in the Isle of Purbeck there was something hereabouts at the time of the Domesday Book [1086]. In particular there are the levelled platforms of ancient house sites on each side of the Corfe River, which separates them with a deep channel. Ploughing has turned up quantities of rough stone rubble, amongst which have been blocks of cut facing-stone which are an indication of something more prestigious.

Boat Knoll – a 250-feet rise topped with a Bronze Age round barrow south-east of East Lulworth, on the south side of the road between the village and Whiteway Hill (SY 867 813). There are other barrows a quarter of a mile to the north-east, which are also just south of the road. All are inside the Lulworth Ranges.

Bond – fraudster **Denis Bond** [died 1746] inherited Creech Grange from his father [1707] and sat in parliament for Poole until he was expelled from the House of Commons for corruption in the clandestine sale of state lands in the Lake District [1720s]. The ill-gotten gains were used to embellish the family seat, with the spending of £1,300 on building work at Creech Grange [1738-41]. Two wings were extended westwards and the south front designed and remodelled by Blandford architect Francis Cartwright.

Denis Bond then built Creech Grange Arch, on top of the Purbeck Hills, and Creech Grange Chapel (see their entries). He is buried in St Michael's Church, Steeple.

Bond – puritan sermon writer **John Bond** [1612-76] co-owned the Lutton estate, between Steeple and Kimmeridge. He was born at Chard, died at Swanage, and is buried in St Michael's Church, Steeple.

Bond – timewarp author **Lilian Bond** [1887-1980], born in Tyneham House, wrote the evocative annals of the mansion and its feudal lost village, which was absorbed into the Lulworth Ranges [1943] and later largely destroyed. She lived in this idyllic village until her marriage to cousin Ivo Bond on the outbreak of the Great War [1914]. *Tyneham: a Lost Heritage* would be published by Henry Longman at the Friary Press, Dorchester [1956].

Bond – lawyer and politician **Sir Nathaniel Bond** [1634-1707] bought the Lutton estate, in the Isle of

Purbeck, from his elder brothers John and William Bond, and then acquired the reversion of Creech Grange estate and mansion from John Lawrence [1686]. It became, and remains, the family seat. Nathaniel Bond was MP for Corfe Castle [1680] and Dorchester [1681], following in the footsteps of his father Denis Bond [died 1658] who had been the town's leading republican – nominated to try King Charles I for high treason.

Nathaniel was appointed Recorder of Weymouth [1683] and his protestant credentials brought their reward after the Glorious Revolution. He became King's Serjeant to William of Orange and was knighted [1693]. He is buried in St Michael's Church at Steeple.

Bond – colonial administrator **Ralph Garneys Bond** [1880-1952] of Tyneham House crossed Russia on the newly constructed Trans-Siberian Railway [1901], joined the Sudan Political Service and shot a Dorcas gazelle with a head of world record size [1913]. He then lived with his pets and faithful servant, Said, and gave a giraffe, Maudie, to London Zoo.

Back home, he married Evelyn Blake [1926], studied bats, and was fated to be the last squire of his beloved Tyneham, being evicted from his manor house to Gardener's Cottage when a coastal radar station was established [1941] and left with his tenants when the entire parish was depopulated for an extension of the Lulworth Ranges [1943].

His exile was spent at Moigne Combe, Owermoigne, where his last public duties were as High Sheriff of Dorset [1945-46] and succeeding his cousin, John Bond, as chairman of Wareham magistrates. The ruination of Tyneham "hurt him terribly". There is now a stone to him in St Mary's churchyard.

Bond's Folly – the local name for Creech Grange Arch. (See its entry).

Botteridge Pool – the old name for Kimmeridge Bay, as it appears on late-mediaeval maps such as that by Ralph Treswell [1585-86]. Association with the village that now provides its name was once less strong as the western half of the bay belongs to the neighbouring parishes of Steeple and Tyneham.

Brandy Bay – uninhabited historically, and since cleared of any nearby population by its inclusion in the Lulworth Ranges [1943], this half-mile sweep of lonely shore (SY 890 795) was given its name in smuggling days. At least one band of smugglers were captured as they hauled their kegs of spirits up the crags of Gad Cliff [1834], with the six being sentenced to death, though this was later reprieved.

The bay has a wide, tumbling undercliff, and is dominated by the conical grass summit of Tyneham Cap, at 520 feet above sea level.

Eastwards of this, above South Egliston, was RAF Brandy Bay, a wartime coastal radar station [established 1941]. Traces of its footings for apparatus remain (SY 900 801) as do some remains of huts, but staff quarters for the operators was the requisitioned Tyneham House.

Broad Bench – classic geological landform of the western offshoot of the Kimmeridge shale ledges, actually in the south-east corner of Tyneham parish (SY 897 787), inside the Lulworth Ranges. Just below the high-tide line is a grey shelf 200 yards wide which projects 150 yards seawards and dries out at low water.

Notorious as a navigation hazard it claimed numerous wrecks until the advent of radar and satellite location. Total losses included the schooner *Liberty*, with all her crew [25-26 September 1868] and the cutter *Ceres*, from which three crewmen had narrow escapes [21 March 1886].

The shelf, which is indeed bench-shaped, is visible from the coast path when the Lulworth Range Walks are open, but does not have closer public access.

Broadmoor Farm – on the heath north-west of Creech Grange, Steeple (SY 900 831), inside the Lulworth Ranges, with an unusual concentration of old roads, being the meeting place for six or more, as Professor Ronald Good has shown. They crossed the brackish stream in a wide droveway that linked Grange Heath with another area of commonable waste on the other side, opening out from a point only sixty yards south of the farmhouse.

Today the farm is ruined and served by no road. But even before the army ranges were extended in 1943 its communications had dropped to a single track that connected with the county-maintained road from Creech to Povington. Broadmoor Farm is a nineteenth century house but its battered sides show signs of earlier cob and stone walling. Professor Good found no reason for its importance apart from the fact that it offered a firm crossing of the small stream that runs from Grange to Hurst Mill.

Brooke – soldier poet **Rupert Brooke** [1887-1915] frequently visited Bournemouth and wrote his immortal words, about "some corner of a foreign field", when he was at Blandford Camp with the Royal Naval Division [1914].

He also stayed in West Lulworth, in rooms above the Post Office. Having noticed "Lulworth" on a map, whilst on holiday with his two maiden aunts at Grantchester Dene, Dean Park Road, Bournemouth, he set out to see the Cove and write verse [1907].

"Tomorrow," he wrote, "I'm going to the most beautiful place in England to work. It is called West Lulworth."

Burngate – the present **Burngate Farm**, north of Lulworth Camp, West Lulworth (SY 836 817) probably incorporates stone from Mount Poynings, a house on the 400-feet contour 100 yards to the north, just east of the

B3071. That was built by Thomas, Lord Poynings in about 1541-46, using stone from Little Bindon, the original Bindon Abbey. The site of Mount Poynings is now an area of disturbed undulations.

The original Burngate or "Brown Gate" was probably a grange of Bindon Abbey, after its move from Lulworth Cove to Wool [1172].

Butts — novelist **Mary Butts** [1890-1937] immortalised the small manor house at South Egliston, Tyneham (SY 899 798), in her writings. It would be incorporated in the Lulworth Ranges [1943] and now stands in ruins, engulfed by luxuriant vegetation spreading across its secluded Gwyle.

Born at Salterns, Lilliput — in a "maggot-knot of dwellings" beside Poole Harbour — she was anguished at the new barbarism that was changing the face of rural England from the cherished Edwardian water-colour vision of her childhood into the harsh mechanised sprawl of the suburbanised Twenties and Thirties. Ironically her most notable bête noire, leading town planner Sir George Pepler, also found his refuge from his own doings beside the Lulworth Ranges, at Little Bindon.

The Castle Inn — late eighteenth century hostelry, from the time when Lulworth and sea-bathing became fashionable, on the north side of the Main Street, West Lulworth, opposite its junction with School Lane (SY 827 808).

The Cat — ruined farmstead on the edge of Povington Heath, Tyneham (SY 874 837), beside the B3070, on the north side of the road, with a strip of land either side of Luckford Lake. Its last occupant, Mrs S.P. Damen, was evicted when the Lulworth Ranges were extended [1943].

Heathcroppers carved this little holding out of former common land. It became a wayside inn when the well-heeled followed the royal example and took to sea-bathing

[1790]. The name came about "as it was known for a big tabby cat which used to sit on the gate".

Ceres — Poole-based cutter, carrying barley up-Channel from Truro, wrecked on Broad Bench [21 March 1886]. One seaman drowned but the other three were eventually saved by the Kimmeridge lifeboat, despite the fact that the sea was sweeping over the deck throughout the rescue.

Charles — ejected French monarch **Charles X** [1757-1836] packed his treasures, assembled his entourage, and departed from Cherbourg. The 73-year-old exile arrived in Poole Harbour on Monday, 23 August 1830, aboard the English steamboat *Comet*.

His reception at the Ballast Quay, Hamworthy, was better than he had feared, and many hats were raised, if only out of polite respect for his age. The Duke of Wellington, the head of the British government, ordered the Custom House authorities at Poole not to inspect any of the king's baggage. Ten days after his arrival, £500,000 was invested in consols and this was only a fraction of the royal wealth: the king must have fled with considerable loot. Thus a coffer of the French state was emptied into London government stock.

Charles had a following of 120 servants and the whole court went from Poole to Lulworth Castle on the edge of Purbeck, where the Roman Catholic Weld family were sympathetic hosts. The guests filled the castle and extra rooms had to be found at Hethfelton House, four miles to the north and standing on the side of a wild hill above the Holy Stream at East Stoke.

At Lulworth, the former king consoled himself by shooting game on the estate preserves and regularly attended mass at the chapel in the castle grounds. He looked out over the sea every day; it was not just any sea but the English Channel, with Cherbourg seventy miles distant though beyond the horizon.

Allowing the monarch to set up home on the South Coast was seen by the government as provocation against France which was liable to encourage an attempt to land and carry off the young Duke of Bordeaux, who was with the king at Lulworth. Diplomatically, Westminster foresaw greater safety and less political embarrassment in moving the entire court to Holyrood at Edinburgh, and the admiralty steam packet *Lightning* arrived at Poole for this purpose on 14 October. Six days later, the king sailed to his northern place of exile.

On leaving Lulworth, there was a gathering in the castle hall when "the English servants knelt to take leave of him" and Charles said "Goodbye, God bless you".

Villagers thronged around his carriage and the newspapers tell of their sorrow. Caustic comments were made at the time: that the cause of their unhappiness was the prospect of a speedy fall in the price of butter, eggs and poultry "for whilst the court was at Lulworth, the farmers' wives of the Isle of Purbeck had got double, and sometimes treble, prices".

Charnel — western corner of Kimmeridge Bay (SY 900 790), actually in the parish of Tyneham and therefore inside the Lulworth Ranges [since 1943].

It may take its name from being a virtual boneyard, due to bodies being frequently washed-up here from shipwrecks on the adjacent Kimmeridge Ledges. *Sharnoll*, however, was Old English for "a dirty well or stream" and could apply here as there is a dependable trickle of fresh-water from the shale rocks immediately south-east of the former Kimmeridge Lifeboat Station (SY 901 791). In order to keep it clean it was dug-out and stone-lined as a cistern and culvert [1868].

Closure of the Lifeboat Station was followed by its use as a small boat-building yard. Anti-invasion defences were constructed here [1940] of which a pill-box survives, on the western cliffs (SY 899 789). It is circular, in concrete, with grooved sides; having been cast into a mould made from hoops of corrugated iron that were intended for use in Nissen huts.

Access to the shore and along the coast path when the Lulworth Range Walks are open.

Churchill — war leader **Winston Churchill** [1874-1965] visited Lulworth Camp as Prime Minister "to see my tanks" when the first operational Churchills were put through their paces by the Gunnery Wing of the Armoured Fighting Vehicles School [6 April 1942]. Wearing a heavy coat, bowler and that famous bulldog look, he inspected massed rows of the new tanks that bore his name, in Halcombe Vale, above Sea Vale Farm, East Lulworth.

Claypits and mines — extensive heathland open-pit workings at West Creech, in the western part of Steeple parish that lies inside the Lulworth Ranges (SY 892 827), produce the finest quality ball clay. This grey clay from the Purbeck heaths has been used by pot-makers since Roman times. Over the past two centuries it became established as the vital bonding agent in the potteries of north Staffordshire and local ceramics works such as Poole Pottery.

Demand for ball clay from Dorset had developed originally when other Staffordshire potters imitated the new skills found by the Wedgwood family and from their studies came salt glazing, the use of moulds, and the realisation that more care had to be taken when selecting clays for their colour and consistency. Ball clay fires white, or near white, when heated in an oxydising atmosphere to between 1,000 and 1,400 degrees Celcius. Poole Pottery is thrown from a mixture principally of ball clay with china clay, flint and Finnish felspar. In 1973 the Purbeck connection lapsed for a while and this ball clay was coming from Newton Abbot as, said department manager Gerry

Webb, “we take our clay from the best seam which English China Clays happen to be operating at the time”.

Initial transportation of ball clay, to Poole Harbour or to weathering beds at Furzebrook, was by a network of narrow gauge mineral railways from 1806 until 1970, originally in horse-drawn wagons.

Having closed their railway, operators Pike-Fayle — who are now part of the minerals conglomerate English China Clays — used lorries to transport clay to the processing works, a collection of sheds covering ten acres in Furzebrook. There are still sidings of the Swanage branch of semi-denationalised British Railways at Furzebrook, but road transport takes most of the clay out of Purbeck. The processing methods crush and shred the clay, remove moisture and put it through various stages of dry mixing, before turning it into a fine powder blown through air flotation mills. After shredding, blending, drying and granulating, the clay is artificially weathered — subjecting it to alternate cutting, soaking, pressure sprays, moving and further soaking. The effect of two years' weather on the clay is achieved in only a matter of weeks.

These processes have greatly speeded the output of clay from Purbeck and with the exploitation of the extensive deposits under the Lulworth Ranges at West Creech, the total quantity leaving Purbeck has doubled since 1950.

There are mines as well as pits. In 1973, Alan Williamson of English China Clays offered to take my colleague Colin Graham and myself into the Adit-type drift-mine then operating under red flag No. 41 and the north-eastern corner of the Lulworth Ranges (SY 905 854).

He drove us across the river to East Holme where the first banks of heathland soil rise out of the Frome meadowlands. Just before the mine, we crossed the humped bridge over the Swanage railway which exists at this point solely as a siding to the company's central processing works. A rough stony track leads off Holme Lane into dense banks of rhododendron and fir at a place known to the map as Squirrel Cottage because somewhere there is an occupied building hidden in the vegetation. The track is firm and narrow with no end that shows from the road.

In this description I'll retain the present tense of 1973 as it has more impact.

Since 1965 it had carried lorries piled with light grey clay. Nothing suggests this leafy path is the access to a mine and there are no signs of its use by lorries. The mine "headgear" is tucked away in the side of the plantation and is unseen and unexpected until the track turns its last corner. Alan Williamson did not say the obvious, and probably it is noticeable only to the intruder, but the visual impact of East Holme mine on the lives of others is nil.

Its headgear smacks of the set for a John Ford western. The top of the shaft was the domain of one man, Hubert Coffin, who in name, looks and voice would fit the role of a prospector in the same western. Hubert has worked twenty-five years in the Purbeck clayfield and when the bell at the top of the shaft rings he operates a winch to haul four loaded wagons at a time up the steep incline (1 in 3½ gradient) from the bottom of the mine. At the top, Hubert empties the clay, depending on its precise type, into one of a row of mid-air bins. Each takes ten tons and when the lorries reverse underneath, the bins are emptied into them. The clay is segregated from the moment of cutting and an instinct by all who handle it, for subtly varying quality, will keep it categorised into grades through each stage of the operation.

Hubert Coffin is the sort of person you don't bother to quote in a notebook but you remember what he said half an hour later.

"It's nice to see the management once in a while," he said to Williamson. "We wouldn't want you to forget that we are here. Any cigarettes or matches?" Mr Williamson, a Gauloise smoker, is excused a search though not without a

"You should know better," which seems to have been delivered as a reprimand to show that innocence is not assumed. A quick professional frisk clears me but instantly reveals Colin Graham's cigarette lighter. "Contraband" is the word used for smoking accessories.

A tube of rusty iron arch-girders leads into the ground, away from the direction of the trees and under the adjoining field, with a 22-inch gauge railway track running on sleepers down the centre. Halfway down, water meets the top of the clay layer and the floor is uncomfortably sticky. But from here the mine is dry and there is not a single drip from the ceiling - one of the advantages of making holes through nature's most plastic and impervious substance.

At the bottom of the shaft, sixty feet below the surface, the railway has catch-points into a siding running parallel to the main line. Here the mine is at its widest, with ample headroom and a roof totally encased with steel, backed by timber. Each truckful of clay is pushed here and left on this section of track. When four are ready, Hubert pulls them up. These loaded trucks are pushed at speed along the underground railway by *runners* who return to the workface (at the moment 300 yards away) with an empty wagon from the siding.

From this winching zone at the foot of the slope a pattern of straight roadways, called *lanes*, spreads into the mine. These run to the workable limits of the deposit and at East Holme cover some 15 acres. They are five feet high and cased at the sides and top by pit-props, which means you walk with a stoop and occasionally tap your helmet on the roof, which is disconcerting but not painful. The only worrying moment is as we freeze and then stand aside as a truck rumbles at speed down the tunnel towards us. We question the ability of a man to push twelve hundredweight of clay along the rails at such a thundering pace and the answer is that the foot of the shaft is the lowest point of the mine so the gradient is on his side. Only the empties have to be pushed.

A new, but distant, noise is that of two men working on the clayface with street-type pneumatic drills fitted with shovel-shaped heads. There were two teams, each of two men, working down beneath East Holme that day but we only saw one team and never even heard the other, which was cutting in another corner of the mine. The average two-man team produces eight tons per man per eight-hour shift.

The usual life of a mine is twelve to fifteen years and East Holme continued production until I was working on this book when it had provided something over 100,000 tons of ball clay.

When we had covered the 300 yards to the workface at the extremity of the mine I forgot Alan Williamson's advice: "If you want to stay popular with a miner, don't shine your lamp straight in his eyes."

The man I blinded was Jack Abbott who lives at Worgret and had been down East Holme since it opened. Jack joined Pike Brothers at Furzebrook in 1937 and is one of the most experienced workers ECC inherited when it bought out the old company. He was working "in the pink" which meant his current location in the mine was amongst grey clay tainted with slight iron staining.

His mate Trevor Seager, aged 20 and living at Corfe Castle, joined ECC "for the money" (ask a silly question) but there must be more in it than that as his brother John works below ground at Ridge. Mining, like quarrying, runs in families in Purbeck.

Jack remembered the wages of the past: "We were the top paid, not now, but then. We used to take home 100 percent more than any other work, years ago when I started. Everyone's caught up now."

The Purbeck claymen have their own variations of mining words. *Stoddle*, mining parlance for a strut between two supports, is *studdle* in the Isle of Purbeck. Underground working in the Purbeck clayfield started in the 1890s at Creech where production continued with Old Grange, a pre-1939 vertical shaft surmounted by wooden headgear, which managed a low rate of production into the 1970s. It was Mr Williamson's "most romantic looking mine".

Ball clay extraction is a highly individual form of mining with its own specialised methods. Each of the mines has its own character and together they cover deposits of clay which, while scattered, extend no wider that the area which would be dug in the North from a single coalmine when they had such things.

Each mine is self-contained with passages driven to the limit of its own *lens* or seam. The major problem is of sand and water overlying the clay but fractures and breakthroughs are a once-a-year occurrence for Mr Williamson.

"First there is gradual seepage through the clay seam as a slight crack opens, and in hours it can swell to two hundred gallons a minute. We use a heather bag which makes a filter and allows water through but retains the sand, forming a dam to hold back the water." The advised natural filter, according to the text-books, is moss, but heather is traditionally used in Purbeck and is more efficient than a fabric filter. Heather also makes the footings for good roadways.

Candles used to flicker through the mines to burn off methane but ventilation has now improved, though miners' safety lamps are still carried. Lignitic material, which gives off methane, is rare in ball clay but there would be more danger from the decaying wood of old excavations if the clay did not close up on disused tunnels. Methane itself is not poisonous but it displaces oxygen and can be explosive in certain conditions and temperatures.

The most surprising thing you learn underground is that the complete maze of tunnels, supports, rails, pipework and every fitting in the mine has been installed by the same men as cut the clay. This back-up system needs as many skills as the actual clay cutting and grading. For instance every piece of timber has to be placed at precisely the right level or the railway will not even work.

It was striking to walk through a whole environment created by the same men who have to work there. Another surprise was to find the atmosphere totally clean and, apart from the sticky patch at the entrance, without mess. Ball clay is a consistently pure rock which handles perfectly. Similarly, the air is fresh. Nowhere in the mine was it stuffy and the constant temperature, something between fifty to fifty-five degrees Fahrenheit, felt comfortable, though possibly on the cool side if you had to stay there. The only lighting was from the miners' lamps but these are ample in such restricted space.

But here lies one problem: some of Mr Williamson's visitors embarrassingly find they suffer claustrophobia and turn back from the top of the shaft. That was a sensation I did not feel at all and I was happy with my new experience. "You start work on Monday, then," old Hubert said back on top. In the refinement of an otherwise hectically cluttered office, we drank coffee from ball clay mugs and the engineer explained the principles of East Holme and the other mines: "There is a hundred foot interval between the main roadways and these are bordered by virgin clay which is left as shaft-pillar protection to hold the roof.

"We take out a six-feet thickness of clay, usually from the bottom of the deposit as the lower levels tend to be purer. Above, there is another fifteen to forty feet of clay and this will inevitably flow into every excavation. When we finish with a passage we fill it with a timber cage so that the roof is supported for the safety of the next workface. In three months the sides will have completely closed in and it will be blocked. Sometimes, in old mining areas, we come across ground that is now solid but in it the old baulk type of timber is perfectly preserved from the mines of fifty years ago. Clay is a perfect seal and it therefore preserves."

The whole operation is carefully planned and timed. A mine starts with its main roadways being pushed to the boundaries of the deposit in every direction. Clay is then systematically removed from the farthest points with the miners working inwards towards the shaft.

"It is a retreat mining system," Mr Williamson said, "and you leave your troubles behind you. Everything is timed so you support the last roadway you are using to bring out the clay."

The effect of mining on the land above may or may not be noticed, even by the landowner: "When you take out six feet of clay, as clay is plastic, it's just going to flow down into the workings. Subsidence happens in all mining though not at this pace. It depends on the overlying strata and the depth of the workings.

"Subsidence is slow in coal mining areas, because there the rock beds fracture and collapse gradually over a long period. In our mining we are much closer to the surface in a far softer substance. We take out six feet of clay at the level of East Holme and this causes four feet of ground subsidence. The ground actually sinks."

Deeper mines, like those around Creech, have less dramatic results because six feet of clay removed at a depth of 150 feet will only cause about a foot of subsidence on the surface. The sinking ground will then be unnoticed as it will drop uniformly and the whole area at the top of the mine — woods, fields, hedges and fences — is visually unaffected.

"It rolls down together, as in natural subsidence, and there are no swallow holes, ponds or anything noticeable."

No mining takes place under roads, railways or buildings because in those cases only slight movement in the earth would cause costly cracks and indefensible legal actions as "everyone has a right of support".

At East Holme negotiations are taking place with the landowner whose field above the mine is sinking. The main depression has become a pond. Alan Williamson looked at it and turned to Hubert: "Do you remember that pond we emptied at Holme Priory? It was full of eels and they were swallowed by ducks actually shaking with the eels inside them. That pit of ours was full of eels."

What happens to ponds like this depends on the reaction of the landowner: "Some are pleased to have a piece of water for duck-shooting instead of fourth-rate agricultural land." In the East Holme case reinstatement may take place and Mr Williamson outlined how land could be filled back: "There is only two inches of top soil in much of this area so you have to save it. We first go in and remove this, and stack it not more than four feet high otherwise you kill the bacteria. Then we would bring in surplus over-burden from elsewhere, level it and replace the top soil.

"There's nothing you cannot do in mining but there are economic restraints. If you had a beautiful house and wanted to take clay from under it you would rightly find yourself with a damn high bill as you would build protection pillars to hold the ground. This would be more expensive that the value of the extraction. So you don't mine under houses."

Eight of the ten mines have electric mains power but East Holme is one of the exceptions. A portable generator provides the power for hydraulic pumps to empty the bins of clay into lorries, a diesel compressor provides air for the pneumatic spades, and the winch has its own diesel motor.

"It is a noisy compressor," Mr Williamson said, "but we are still surrounded by snakes, deer, squirrels and every

bird under the sun. They are used to the place being here."
Listen, was the instruction from Hubert. He was right — against all the drone you could still hear bird-song. As we departed, Hubert left us with another illusion — that of backwoods nature watcher Henry David Thoreau — as he disappeared to his hut in the trees.

Comrades — film by Skreba Productions, written and directed by Bill Douglas, on the trial and transportation of Dorset's Tolpuddle Martyrs [1834]. Its scenes of village England were re-created among the ruins of Tyneham [1985-86], inside the Lulworth Ranges. Plaster-board and ready-made sections of thatch revamped Post Office Row and a village green took shape on the open ground between St Mary's Church and Gould's Cottage.

Its centrepiece, under which the six "Dorsetshire Labourers" met, was a sycamore — the species on Tolpuddle Green — brought in the scoop of a bulldozer from the Heath Range at Povington. It would survive for three years. *Victims of Whiggery* author George Loveless was the film's hero.

Coombe Keynes — parish of 2,006 acres and small village on the western edge of the Isle of Purbeck, beside the Lulworth Ranges, with the second element of the name being spoken as Kaynes, which shows a long memory for correct pronuciation. The family name is spelt *Chaynes* or *Kaynes* in documents from 1286 onwards and seems not to have been mis-spelt by mapmakers until the first edition of the Ordnance Survey in 1811.

Court Close, the now open ground south and south-east of Holy Rood Church, has extensive settlement remains which centre around a pond. In all they spread over twenty acres, including the adjoining South Close, and amounted to a reasonably sizable village in the Middle Ages. Most dwellings had been deserted by the time of the Hearth Tax assessments, when the village had only fourteen households [1662-64] and a plan shows the site was then almost totally abandoned [1770].

Coombe Keynes chalice — to see the prize possession of the little community of Coombe Keynes you will need a one-day Travelcard. For the village's rare and beautiful silver chalice, dating from about 1500, was loaned to the Victoria and Albert Museum in 1930 and is still there, now being on permanent show in the display of mediaeval church plate. It was originally taken to London for an exhibition of English Mediaeval Art and the parish was provided with a replica in 1931.

The original is one of twenty that are known of the same basic design, with a conical bowl on a hexagonal stem, descending to a Gothic knot of six complex lobes and then into a spreading mullet-shaped base. Of these specimens, dated between 1404 and 1507, the Coombe Keynes example is the simplest and shows the design to perfection. It is six and three-eighths inches high and weighs ten ounces.

Only two other items of pre-Reformation church plate survive in Dorset. Indeed there are only seventy-eight mediaeval chalices in the whole of England. That from Coombe Keynes is undoubtedly one of the finest and most valuable.

Coombe Keynes parish church — the village has shrunk northwards away from Holy Rood, which now stands on a limb, beside a track into the fields (SY 843 841), and was in 1858 in a state of collapse.

"I have never seen a sadder case than this of ecclesiastical dilapidation and difficulty," its surveyor reported. "A portion of the church is a complete ruin and the rest is little better."

The collapsing church of the Holy Rood was rebuilt in 1861 and has an attractive pyramidal roof of Purbeck stone slates on its tower. Its three bells, by Thomas Hey [about

1355], John Wallis [inscribed "Love God, I.W. 1599"], and Anthony Bond ["Anthony Bond made me, 1636"] now hang in Wool church.

The principal feature inside the church is a low, semicircular chancel arch of the twelfth century that probably survives from the original Norman church.

The simple Purbeck stone font had the distinction of having been drawn by Thomas Hardy on 8 April 1861 when he was twenty-one and working for the Dorchester architect John Hicks. The font was moved from the south aisle to the north door. Then in 1979 it was moved again, as Christopher Scoble told me – "to the dismay of the villagers, the font was prised up and removed to the custody of Wool church, where it now stands as a mere museum piece, needlessly divorced from its true historical context".

Holy Rood church was declared redundant by the Church Commissioners and in 1981 it was handed to the Coombe Keynes Trust which was organised by Mrs D.M. Desoutter to ensure its preservation for the community.

Cove Hotel – the main Victorian contribution to visitor-care at Lulworth Cove, at the point where the Main Road becomes a fishermen's cul-de-sac (SY 823 800).

Creech Barrow Hill – to give its local name, the most conspicuous hill in these parts not being graced with one by the Ordnance Survey, rises like the cone of an extinct volcano (SY 922 824). Not that it is, and nor is it an offshoot of the chalk ridge of the Purbeck Hills which lie immediately to the south, a mile east of the Lulworth Ranges.

In fact it is an upswelling, to 634 feet, of the sands, gravels and clays of Purbeck's Great Heath and overlooks the adjoining chalklands at Stonehill Down.

"Creech" is one of the few placenames in Dorset that has descended directly from a Celtic word, that for hill.

Similarly "Barrow" is Saxon for a rounded hill. So the full title of Creech Barrow Hill is etymological three-stage repetition meaning "Hill Hill Hill".

On top, on closer inspection, there turn out to be twin peaks in near proximity, one with a bracken-covered Bronze Age round barrow burial mound. The other, the true summit, has a mound with the foundation walling of a small stone building.

This was a hunting lodge, said to have been built by King John when the Isle of Purbeck was the favourite royal game reserve. It was a rough tower, constructed as a lookout over the heath towards Wareham and Corfe Castle, and is shown as "The Lodge" on John Speed's 1610 map of Dorsetshire.

Creech Grange — Tudor mansion built by Sir Oliver Lawrence on former Bindon Abbey lands [circa 1545], standing to the east side of what are now the Lulworth Ranges (SY 912 823). It was extended on the north side in about 1600.

The Lawrence shields-of-arms are on panels in the barrel-vaulted roof of the parish church of Steeple, showing Lawrence quartering Washington and with initials "D.L.E." and crest. The Washington crest and Edward Washington's initials, dated 1616, appear in the church porch, linking the family with the first American president, George Washington [1732-99].

The other lasting name arrived in 1691 when Nathaniel Bond bought Creech Grange.

Creech Grange Arch — known locally as Bond's Folly, this stands at 625 feet on the Purbeck Hills to the east of the Lulworth Ranges (SY 912 818).

It is an early eighteenth century "eye-catcher" designed to appear above the trees of the Great Wood at Creech as a castle silhouetted on the skyline of the Purbeck Hills, when viewed from the Grange country house below. In reverse, from the hill, the view is framed by the stone arch. The single length of wall of grey Purbeck stone is castellated and studded with little pyramids. It was built by Denis Bond, the owner of Creech Grange [circa 1742], and stands in an acre of hilltop that was given to the National Trust by J.W.G. Bond [1942].

There was an intellectual folly as well as the physical one. Since I started writing about Purbeck in the Dorset County Magazine at the end of the 1960s I have done my best to keep alive the local name, Bond's Folly, as it was in danger of being completely eclipsed by the Ordnance Survey's insistence — as a sop to a former landowner of the Grange — on the less revealing "Grange Arch". The reason for the family's embarrassment was that the term "Bond's Folly" had a double meaning and would originally have been used with a chuckle.

For Denis Bond's folly in life was not this arch but the major corruption scandal of the 1720s when he was expelled from the House of Commons, where he sat as a member for Poole, for insider-dealing by "fraudulently and clandestinely" contracting to sell state-owned lands in the Lake District for much less than they were worth.

Access from the A351 is by taking the road to Kimmeridge. Climb to the top of Purbeck Hills and park in the Creech picnic area on the brow of the hill. Walk eastwards (away from the army range red flags Nos. 50 and 51) for a mile along the prehistoric ridgeway which survives as an attractive green lane along the hog's back of the Purbeck Hills.

Creech Grange Chapel — dedicated to St John and built in the grounds of Creech Grange, north of the mansion and its outbuildings (SY 911 824), by Denis Bond [1746]. Of interest for the chancel arch and other twelfth century stonework recovered from the ruin of Holme Priory, in the adjoining parish of East Holme (SY 898 859).

Denis Bond died before the work was finished and his successors ignored it, using the shell of the building as a carpenters' shed, until John Bond completed it almost a century later. His stained glass memorial window records this, and his own demise a little later: "THIS CHAPEL WAS FITTED UP AT THE EXPENSE OF JOHN BOND OF CREECH ESQ., AS A CHAPEL OF EASE TO THE PARISH OF STEEPLE AD 1840. HE SURVIVED THIS GOOD WORK ONLY FOUR YEARS AND DIED ON MARCH 18th 1844."

The north transept was added by his brother, Rev Nathaniel Bond [1849], serving as an aisle "for the use of the children of the Sunday School", and as a memorial to his eldest son, John Bond, who died that year [8 February 1849]. The pyramidal roof of the west tower was topped off with an elegant classical cupola and the chapel was then consecrated [1859].

Daggers Gate – exciting-sounding placename for the spot on the downs 300 yards north of Newlands Farm where the road to Winfrith Newburgh converges with an untarred public lane from West Down Farm and West Lulworth bridleways numbers 12 and 13 (SY 811 814). Actually it is probably named for someone called Dagger, rather than the weapon, but it does have literary associations as the novelist Thomas Hardy used it for his location Dagger's Grave in *The Distracted Preacher* [1879].

Hardy moved its location, southwards to the cliffs of Man o' War Cove (SY 809 802).

The earliest use of the name seems to be on the parish tithe map [1843].

The Doll's House – dainty eighteenth century timber and plaster single living-room cottage with two miniature bedrooms upstairs, on the south side of Main Road, West Lulworth, after it becomes a cul-de-sac to Lulworth Cove (SY 823 800).

Dudgeon — drowned cook **Robert Dudgeon** [1848-77] has his gravestone in the south-east corner of the old churchyard beside Main Street, West Lulworth: "IN AFFECTIONATE REMEMBRANCE OF ROBERT DUDGEON OF TEDDINGTON, MIDDLESEX, COOK ON BOARD THE SHIP *AVALANCHE* OF LONDON, WHO WAS DROWNED THROUGH HER FOUNDERING AFTER BEING IN COLLISION WITH THE SHIP *FOREST OF WINDSOR* IN THE ENGLISH CHANNEL. SEPTEMBER 1877." She was Canadian; from Windsor, Nova Scotia.

Durdle Door — the tall rock-arch of upturned Portland stone at the west end of a bastion of these hard rocks that has survived the cliff breaches made by the sea on each side (SY 805 802), a mile west of Lulworth Cove car-park. It is open to the south-westerly gales and a little bay is developing on the landward side, between it and the chalk cliffs of Newlands Warren.

"Durdle" is derived from the Old English "thyrel" or "thirl", meaning holed; initial "th" sound being pronounced "d" in the Dorset dialect. At the west side of Newlands Warren the fault-line of the Purbeck Hills (which extends westward to here via Bindon Hill and Hambury Tout) finally reaches the sea. On the east side, just above sea level in St Oswald's Bay, there is a vein of marble in the cliff.

Earl's Kitchen — open heathland, between tank firing points 'M' and 'N' in the Lulworth Ranges (SY 875 829), north of Povington in the parish of Tyneham. Its name is believed to be an allusion to the Earl of Hertford, who was granted the manor of Povington [1582], in jest at a failed attempt to reclaim the heath for a market garden.

More likely the project was undertaken by the previous owner, the Duke of Somerset, because he took some interest in the property, whereas Hertford split up the manor and sold it to the tenants.

Either way it is now featureless apart from one Bronze Age burial mound, 100 yards south-east of tank hard-standing 'N', and bounded west by the brackish waters of Luckford Lake. There is no public access.

East Holme – a parish but hardly a village, more a small country estate, covering 1,067 acres between the River Frome and Holme Heath. That is inside the Lulworth Ranges [since 1943]. The ancient Holme Priory [founded 1170] has its name perpetuated by the present Holme Priory, on the site, which was built by Nathaniel Bond [1770].

St John's parish church, 130 yards east (SY 899 859), includes some stone of the original Cluniac monks but is the work of builders Wellspring and Son of Dorchester to plans by architect John Hicks [1865-66]. A brass memorial to Richard Sidways [1612] has survived from the previous church.

The nearby lane goes through an attractive ford beside Holme Farm (SY 896 859). Southwards, running from west to east, is Holme Lane, which is the only other road through the parish. In places it still lives up to its Saxon name, *holme* being the old word for holly, but much has been ousted by introduced rhododendron which flourishes in the wild on these thin sand and gravel soils.

Both are equally picturesque though the lane now has lesser water-splashes and is wider than its picture postcard state in Edwardian times.

East Holme Rifle Range – leased by the Ministry of Defence as an extension north-east from its Lulworth Ranges, beside East Holme public bridleway number 3 and Army red flag no. 61 (SY 912 849). It is the oldest military facility in Dorset that is still in regular use. Shown on Victorian maps as an 800-yard range [1886].

The rifle range lies between East Holme Farm and the ruin of Dorey's Cottage (SY 912 848), both of which are beside the bridleway. Needless to say, apart from that path, there is no public access and the area south-west of the butts is out of bounds "for all purposes" to military personnel as well.

East Lulworth – parish of 2,311 acres, including the estate-owned thatched village of the same name, and adjacent Lulworth Park with the shell of Lulworth Castle. Seawards the parish and the view from the castle battlements extends to Flower's Barrow and the Arish Mell gap into Worbarrow Bay. Eastward from here the land is leased for tank firing [since 1923] and westwards likewise by the extension of the Lulworth Ranges [1943].

Inland the parish also stretches into the Lulworth Ranges, where the former Lulworth Heath is no longer common land and now half covered by pine trees (SY 872 838).

East Lulworth parish church – St Andrew's stands in Lulworth Park, less than a hundred yards south of Lulworth Castle (SY 854 821). The oldest part of the building is the "very large embattled tower" of the fifteenth century, supported at the corners by huge buttresses. Distanced now from its re-located village [1780-85] and surrounded by the park of the Roman Catholic Weld family. This Anglican church, however, long pre-dates both the castle and the Welds, with a vicars' list that goes back centuries [to 1312].

Rebuilding in 1788 removed the rest of the "ancient fabric, built in the style of the Norman architecture" apart from the west end of the mediaeval north wall which retains what church historian Fred Pitfield identifies as "fifteenth century casement moulded jambs, sill and part of the mullion of the north-west window".

The 1788 walls came together as a semi-circular apse, which stylistically supports the theory that the architect was John Tasker who also built the nearby Catholic church [1786-87] for landowner Thomas Weld, paymaster of both projects.

Victorian restoration, by Dorchester architect John Hicks, followed in 1863-64 and amounted to almost total rebuilding of the nave and chancel. The latter lost its apse and was extended into a conventional squared-up east end. Wellspring and Son, builders from Dorchester, resurrected the mediaeval floor-plan: "In clearing away the ground the foundations of the old chancel were discovered and the new one has been carried out to the same extent."

East Lulworth Village – formerly extended westwards to the fifteenth century parish church of St Andrew's (SY 854 821), until the refurbishment of Lulworth Castle and removal of its formal gardens and nearby cottages for replacement by the newly laid-out park [1773-85].

The only other building to survive, apart from the castle and the church, was the Stable Courtyard (SY 855 821) but this was almost completely rebuilt and given a new datestone [1777].

Now the most westerly of the buildings in the present village is a seventeenth century cottage near the southern junction between the old main street and its by-pass for tanks (SY 857 818). Most of the other twenty or so thatched cottages to the north-west (SY 858 819 to 862 825) were provided by the Weld family for servants and estate staff who were displaced by the destruction of their homes to make way for the creation of the park [1773].

Ten acres of banks, hollows and house-platforms mark the site of the original village, south of the Stables (SY 855 820) and old maps show meadows on the north side of these buildings.

Egliston – known locally as *Eggleston*, inside the Lulworth Ranges with South Egliston being one of the least known of the Gwyles, the deep-cut wooded glens on the Purbeck coast. The popular name is purest; derived from that of the owner of the land, between Tyneham and Kimmeridge, at the time of King John – one Engelini or Egelin. The name is given as *Eggleston* on Isaac Taylor's map of 1765.

Apparently the most romantic of today's ruins on these tank firing ranges, despite stone-robbing in the late 1960s, the small manor house at South Egliston (SY 899 798) was immortalised in the writings of Mary Butts [1890-1937]. It was a rural idyll, which enthused her into outbursts against the new barbarism that was tarnishing her childhood Edwardian water-colour vision of England, replacing it with the harsh mechanised sprawl of the suburbanised Twenties and Thirties.

English – comedian **Arthur English**, who rose to fame as the "Wide Boy" and became known through the "Variety Bandbox" programme to radio listeners across the globe, was an instructor in the Gunnery Wing of the Armoured Fighting Vehicles School at Lulworth Camp.

"It's nice to think that the boys at Lulworth still remember me," he told The Tank magazine. "A lot of water's passed under the bridge since I was there – some of it pretty chilly. But I don't have to run to Wool to catch the Passion Wagon to Bournemouth any more, and it seems a long time since I had a pint at The Castle.

"I had a rough time when I came out of the Army. I was navvying on the roads for six months until I got a job as a painter at Aldershot, but all the time I was trying to get a break into show business. My chance didn't come until I got an audition at the Windmill and Mr Vivian van Damm (O.C., Windmill Girls) gave me a job on the spot. I've been resident comedian there ever since and I can tell you that the faces you see in the Windmill canteen are a lot easier on the eye than some of those I remember in the Sergeants' Mess at Lulworth."

Fishing — shellfish were the speciality catch in these waters.

George Wellstead operated fishing boats at Worbarrow in the nineteenth century and was the major Wareham dealer in lobsters and crabs. There was an oyster pond in the western arc of Lulworth Cove.

Walter Miller, who was born in 1890, told me in 1971 about the old-time fishing industry of Purbeck, Lulworth and Ringstead. He was once advised by his friend the writer Llewelyn Powys: "When you see an old man, ask him all you can." This I did when I was with Miller and he explained how the old fishermen lived and worked by pot-fishing in the shallow offshore waters:

"Lobsters used to be caught more than crabs, as those change their skins and are slim before they do so. The saying is that crabs are good when there is an 'r' in the month. But in May, June and July they aren't much good.

"There was fifteen fishermen at Lulworth, and now there's only two. There were around six at Worbarrow. There was Jack and Tom, and another called Tarry and his mate, and then there was old Charlie. All were one family originally but Henry Miller, the last one, had two sons, Jack and Tom, and both died during the war after the occupation [by the military in 1943].

"At Ringstead the catch was rowed to Weymouth. That at Worbarrow was taken by fishmongers who used to come down over Tyneham Hill from Wareham. They came the same to Lulworth. Father and them, when they couldn't come, they carried their catch on their backs to Weymouth and that was never considered any trouble. The fishmongers at Wareham, when they had too much, put what was over into a packing case. The lobsters were live with seaweed over them. They put them on a fast passenger train to London and they were sold at Billingsgate.

"When mother had two lobsters, a pound-and-a-half, she would cook them, cool them down, put them in a basket and I'd take them and sell them at ninepence a pound. That made your mouth water! Everyone would have a feed of lobster sometimes. Good sirloin beef was then eightpence a pound. Visitors would come down and get the lobsters fresh, cooked on spatches.

"All these fishermen were rabbit catchers in the winter. They had to because you couldn't make a living out of fishing alone, as you couldn't earn enough; there wasn't enough gear. Sixty pots was as much as you could do. Now they work four hundred and the Lulworth Grounds, a huge triangular shape off Lulworth, is prime fishing. They come up from Swanage and down from Brixham. But the lobsters aren't there now and we consider it's overfished. In the old days everything had a chance to live."

Five Barrows — actually six magnificently preserved Bronze Age round barrows inside the Lulworth Ranges in a straight line on a rise in the heathland midway between the Heath Gate and West Holme Heath on the road across the army ranges from East Lulworth to Holmebridge, in the north-west corner of Tyneham parish (SY 875 840). A nearby milestone used to read "London 117, Lulworth 2" and the extended hillock rises from Povington Heath a mile west of Hurst Mill to overlook the undergrowth that hides Luckford Lake.

Flower's Barrow — hill-fort entrenchments inside the Lulworth Ranges, across the western extremity of the Purbeck Hills, taking full advantage of precipitous 565-feet high chalk cliff above Worbarrow Bay (SY 864 805). No defences were necessary along this southern side. This is the only Iron Age fortification in Purbeck and it appears to be of a late date, about 50 BC.

It now encloses only about four acres but at least half as much again must have fallen over the cliff. There are strong double banks on the landward approaches with the spaces between the ramparts being stretched at the west and east ends to keep the advantage of height over distance constantly with the defenders. The inner rampart at the east side stands six feet higher than the outer bank. These were key requirements for their slingstone weaponry. Pebbles for slingstones were found in a 1939 excavation.

Depressions mark the sites of underground grain stores. It is likely that Flower's Barrow was stormed by the Romans in AD 43-44, though a much fuller excavation would be necessary to prove that. A decapitated skeleton of "great stature" was found in the nineteenth century on the inner rampart.

Flower's Barrow is accessible only when the Lulworth Range Walks are open, and unless you approach from the Povington Hill car-park (SY 888 812) you will find it a stiff climb.

Fossil Forest – the national treasure of the Lulworth Ranges, on the slanting ledges above the sea between Lulworth Cove and Mupe Bay, literally in the splash-zone during strong winds (SY 832 797). The line of cycad tree stumps is accessible by foot from Lulworth Cove, via Little Bindon, but only when Lulworth Range Walks are open.

The three best tree trunks are at the extreme eastern end of the ledges, which involves a little minor rock clambering about half-way along. They are hollow at the core and about six feet across. No longer vertical, they tilt with the strata at about forty-five degrees towards the cliff-top. One pair grew about ten feet apart.

A notice board is informative: "Many of the rocks of Purbeck began as sediments accumulating 120 million years ago in swamps. As the soils gradually built up, large pine-like and fern-like trees grew here. Some of these stumps became fossilised, but only the former positions of the stumps, covered by a lime-type deposit, can now be seen. The Fossil Forest is part of a site of special scientific interest. It is an important part of our heritage and deserves your care, consideration and protection."

In other words the stumps are only the shapes of the trees – not fossilised wood. Geological vandals who attack them with hammers to remove souvenirs take away meaningless bits of calcareous tufa.

French privateer – in 1694 King William III presented Captain Peter Joliffe of Poole with a gold medal and chain for his boldness in attacking with his hoy a French privateer that was three times his strength. He had seen it capturing a Weymouth boat that was fishing the Lulworth grounds.

Joliffe not only forced the enemy to release his prize but forced him to beach near Lulworth where the local people took the crew prisoner.

The medal was inscribed: "His Majesty's Gift as a reward to Peter Joliffe of Poole, for his good service against the enemy in retaking a Ketch of Weymouth from a French privateer, and chasing the said privateer on Shore near Lulworth in the Isle of Purbeck, where he was broken in pieces." [London Gazette, 3089.]

There would be another hero in the family. St James's church in Poole has a plaque to Peter Slade Joliffe of the Royal Air Force who was killed in action in Norway in 1940.

Gad Cliff – multiple limestone crags, tilted skyward at the precipitous seaward edge as a crinkle-cut overhang to a mile of tumbling undercliff, eastward from Worbarrow Tout to Brandy Bay (SY 872 795 to 892 796). Landward of the lip, overlooking Tyneham Valley, is the coastal path of the Lulworth Range Walks.

"Gad" takes its name from a quarryman's wedge and perfectly describes its dramatic angular shape. These outcrops climax at 435 feet. Below, midway along the shore and about a thousand yards east of Pondfield Cove, is the Wagon Rock.

The undercliff here is of considerable width, being more than a hundred yards, and varies between active scree slopes — from the crags crumbling from above — to grassy ribs of consolidated ground

It provides a traditional eyrie for the peregrine falcon; one of only a handful in southern Britain that continued to function through the 1960s and 70s when populations crashed to near-extinction due to toxic agricultural chemicals.

Grange Gate Lake — between Old Bond Street and the Breach Plantation, north-east of Creech Grange (SY 914 830), being the water-filled hole that was dug by Pike Brothers of Furzebrook for ball clay [1896-1914]. It was a large working and created the largest of the heathland lakes in the Isle of Purbeck, being 900 feet long by 250 feet across.

A narrow-gauge mineral railway, from Furzebrook Works and weathering-beds, crossed Grange Road midway between Old Bond Street and Breach Cottages (SY 916 831). The wagons were hauled by steam engine. The first of them, *Primus*, was replaced by *Quartus* as work developed on the Grange Gate pit [1899], and the other two little locomotives were *Secundus* and *Tertius*.

Nothing industrial has survived. There is just water, surrounded by impenetrable vegetation, except for a short length of grassy bank on the east side. Here the lake is passed by Steeple public bridleway number 2 and the spot is usually occupied by Canada geese.

Gwyle — Cornish word for uncultivated ground, introduced to the Isle of Purbeck by the Williams family from Probus when they bought Tyneham House in 1567. It is used for wooded glens between Tyneham Village and Worbarrow; at

South Egliston; and north and south of Encombe House. Though all these are coastal situations, the name also occurs inland, immediately north of Rempstone Hall, on the other side of Corfe Castle.

Hambury Tout – rounded hill above the cliffs west of Lulworth Cove, topped at 454 feet above sea level by a Bronze Age bell barrow (SY 816 803).

This burial mound is about 80 feet in diameter and ten feet high and is probably that opened by John Milner, recorded in the Gentleman's Magazine [1790], who found "at Hambury Toote" a large pile of ashes beneath a central cairn of stones. Above this lay a contracted skeleton with an urn placed on its chest.

The name itself is of some antiquity. "Hambury" means, probably, "high barrow", and "Tout" was "a lookout".

William Lisle Bowles observed in his *Dissertation on the Celtic Deity Tutes* [1828] that "most of the hills of the sea-coast, and through Dorsetshire, are still pronounced Teuts [Toots] by the common people". These days it is generally pronounced as it is spelt. Alternatively, though only by Victorian visitors, Worbarrow Tout was occasionally called Worbarrow Knob.

Hannay – holidaymaker **James Owen Hannay** [1865-1950] was inspired by his stay at Lulworth Cove, in September 1923, to write the novel *Bindon Parva*. In it a Purbeck priest celebrates communion, at Steeple, with unseen dead parishioners from across the centuries. A parson himself, Hannay published it under the pseudonym George A. Birmingham [1925]. Further information: consult *Literary Dorset*.

Hardy – novelist **Thomas Hardy** [1840-1928] not only used Lulworth Cove, thinly disguised as Lulwind Cove, for several dramatic incidents, but also worked on building the new West Lulworth parish church [1869] to plans produced by his late employer, Dorchester architect John Hicks.

Harp Stone – ancient standing stone, in a hedgerow in the valley of the Corfe River south-east of Steeple village, a mile east of the Lulworth Ranges (SY 922 806). It is an upright limestone monolith over seven feet tall, on the bank of a small stream and on the western edge of a narrow coppice. Romantic writers have taken the name to be for "the harp player's stone".

The farmhouse of Hurpstone, an eighteenth century building, lies roofless and ruinous 400 yards to the east. Surrounding it are the remains of earlier desertion, the mediaeval settlement of the place called *Harpera* or *Herpere* in the Domesday Book [1086]. It was not recorded as *Herpston* until 1340, so there is nothing in the place-name evidence to support a claim of great antiquity for the stone. Having said that, it is deeply grooved by weathering, and could date from anywhere between the Bronze Age and Saxon times.

Surviving as it does, in a hedgerow, it may be the only remnant of a row or alignment that has otherwise been destroyed.

Holme Mount – rounded lesser summit of the western Purbeck heaths, belittled by Creechbarrow Hill, a mile south-east of East Holme (SY 906 844). Its gently rounded top rises to 210 feet, with two Bronze Age round barrows and Army red flag no. 43 on top.

It is doubly out-of-bounds, at all times, being inside the Lulworth Ranges [since 1943] and also in the overshoot area behind East Holme rifle range. The conifer stands west of Bridewell Plantation now encroach on the eastern and southern slopes, reducing the former immensity of the heath.

This used to be of agricultural importance for turning out stock, and the right to drive cattle here, annually on

Whit Sunday, was customarily exercised by the people of Corfe Castle to keep open their access to the commonable heaths.

Holme Priory — a cell of Cluniac monks, administrated by Montacute Abbey, Somerset, in turn owing direct allegiance to Cluniac Abbey in France, established in the meadows of the River Frome, north of what are now the Lulworth Ranges (SY 899 859) in about 1130. After Henry VIII's dissolution of the monasteries [1539] it became the parish church for East Holme and remained in use until 1715.

The ancient building then fell into ruin. A remarkably fine chancel arch, contemporary with the original church, was then rescued from the ruins and rebuilt in the chapel being constructed at Creech Grange [1746].

Eventual clearance of the site [1865] was followed by the building of a neat church, of heathstone with Hamstone corners and bellcote, at the expense of landowner Nathaniel Bond, in memory of his younger brother: "THIS CHURCH IS ERECTED AD 1865 TO THE GLORY OF GOD AND IN MEMORY OF DENIS WILLIAM BOND obiit JANUARY 23rd 1863."

The architect was John Hicks of Dorchester and the builders, Wellspring and Son, were also from the county town. Its highly pointed style, for windows, arches and gables, is Early English. The dedication is to St John.

The stone of the interior arches is from Bath and Ham Hill, in alternate courses. The mouldings and carvings were by Bolton of Worcester, the Dorset County Chronicle recorded after the consecration celebrations of 12 April 1866: "Running round the interior is a bold cornice of Bath stone beautifully carved in floriated pattern; and the corbels in the nave have small Purbeck marble shafts terminating in bosses, some of them bearing shields, with coats of arms, being those of the ancient owners of the estate, commencing with that of Alfred de Lincoln, by whom it was conveyed to the Priory of Montacute, and terminating with the present owner."

These shields were the work of Lady Selina Bond, the wife of Nathaniel Bond, who also painted the illuminated texts above the windows and the chancel arch.

A brass on the west wall, to Richard Sidwayne who died aged 63, on 2 November 1612, is from the earlier church and was found on its site during the planting of trees in 1812. An eighty acre park was created at East Holme and Holme Priory was resurrected as the name for its mansion.

Kadow — Luftwaffe pilot **Oberleutnant Gerhard Kadow**, in a Messerschmitt of the 9th Staffel, Zerstörergeschwader-76, was the first German to be brought down and taken prisoner in the Battle of Britain, on Povington Heath, Tyneham — inside what are now the Lulworth Ranges — on 11 July 1940:

"I flew Me110 number 2N + EP, with my wireless operator and air gunner, Gefreiter Helmut Scholz. My squadron was stationed at Laval, and we flew from there to Dinard for refuelling and from Dinard to England at about 12.00 noon.

"My squadron, together with two others, had orders to protect Ju 87 Stuka dive-bombers, which would attack targets on the South Coast of England in the vicinity of Portland.

"Before we started, our commander Major Grabmann, told us that it was vital that no Stuka be lost. This meant a considerable risk to our lives.

"At the English coast I counted some twenty dark spots in the distance, somewhat higher than we were. I was certain they were RAF fighters, but couldn't recognise whether they were Hurricanes or Spitfires — but knew that our twin-engined machines were no match for these single-engined fighters.

"However, it was our duty to protect the Stukas, so that they could bomb unhindered. The main strength of the

Me110 was the two 20mm cannons and four machine guns in its nose. I pressed the firing buttons and bullets flew like water out of a watering can towards the enemy. The closing speed was high, and at the last minute both I and my attacker had to break away to avoid a head-on collision. Whether I scored any hits or not, I don't know.

"The next moment, two fighters were on my tail and had opened fire. Almost immediately both of my engines stopped and a return to the Continent was clearly impossible. The enemy saw his success and stopped shooting, but watched me from behind.

"I flung off my cabin roof for a quick escape and hoped it would hit him. I ordered Helmut Scholz to do the same. He radioed that the mechanism to ditch his cabin roof would not operate as a result of bullet damage.

"I couldn't bail out and leave Scholz to his fate, and for the same reason a ditching in the sea seemed unwise. The only alternative was a crash landing on British soil.

"After we had landed I found I could not leave my cockpit — a high explosive bullet had hit my seat causing a big hole. The torn aluminium 'fangs' around the hole had nailed themselves through my parachute pack and tunic and onto my flesh.

"I pulled myself forward, and suddenly was free. I left the aircraft and smashed the cabin roof of my gunner so that he could get out. He was hurt only by shell splinters. The first thing to do was destroy the aircraft. We didn't have a self-destruct charge, so opened the fuel caps and tried to ignite the petrol with the muzzle flash from my pistol.

"I fired eight shots, but had no success. In hindsight, this was just as well, otherwise the aircraft would have exploded and killed us."

Keats — poet **John Keats** [1795-1821] apparently spent his last hours on English soil at Lulworth Cove when the *Maria Crowther* put in whilst en route for Italy, on 30

September 1820. It was during this brief Dorset interlude, whilst Captain Walsh waited for a favourable wind, that he is said to have regained his composure and written his final poem, the sonnet "Bright star, would I were steadfast as thou art."

Maria Crowther was outward bound, and Captain Walsh was waiting for a favourable wind, and thought it wise to let his passengers go on shore at intervals to improve their morale.

The landing place has been subject to conjecture, with Studland Bay and Holworth at Ringstead having their supporters, but tradition, boosted by a poem from Thomas Hardy, favours Lulworth. Hardy's centenary poem of September 1920 asks, "You see that man?" and answers:

"That man goes to Rome — to death, despair;
And no one notes him now but you and I:
A hundred years and the world will follow him there,
And bend with reverence where his ashes lie."

Kimmeridge Lifeboat Station — in a gully at Charnel, beside Kimmeridge Bay, in the south-east corner of Tyneham parish (SY 901 791). Established after a series of shipwrecks along this shore, [1868] with William Stickland, of Stickland's Cottage, South Egliston, being coxswain of its boat, the 28-feet *Mary Heape*.

He was the hero of the rescue of seventeen men crewing the stricken Norwegian vessel *Stralsund*, which wedged on the Kimmeridge Ledges in ferocious seas [8-9 December 1872].

Immediately after William Stickland's death [March 1881] the boat was replaced by the 32-feet *Mary Heape II*. She saved three seamen from the cutter *Ceres*, from Poole [21 March 1886] and continued in service until 1887.

The next and final boat was the 34-feet *Augustus Arkwright* which would succeed in refloating the brigantine *Lythemore* [26 June 1892].

The station had its limitations, particularly because of its distance from the far-flung dwellings of this sparsely-populated shore, and shortage of manpower caused its closure [1896].

Its large shed and slipway became a boat-building yard, operated by Louis Stickland, son of the late William. It now lies inside the Lulworth Ranges [since 1943] and has been reduced to footings and the remains of the rails and the winch. Fresh water trickles into the sea, out of the cliff to the south-east, and was intercepted by a stone-built culvert.

There is a path down through the gully from the main coast path of the Lulworth Range Walks, when these are open, or alternatively across the rocks from Kimmeridge Bay.

Kimmeridge Oil Well — on the low shale cliffs above Kimmeridge Bay, actually in the parish of Steeple, beside the coast footpath (SY 904 793). Immediately outside the south-east corner of the Lulworth Ranges, beside red flag No. 56.

British Petroleum's "nodding donkey" or pump-jack oilwell was the first successful drilling in what is now the Purbeck oil-field. It has been pumping since 1959, from the Cornbrash limestone at 1,790 feet, and cumulative production is now in the region of half a million tons.

That is almost a drop in the ocean — a poor-taste metaphor when it comes to crude oil — in terms of North Sea production and even its sister series of wells that came on-line south of Poole Harbour after Wytch Farm oil-site "X" for exploration struck black gold in the autumn of 1973.

The Lake — Joseph Weld had the valley dammed to the north of Home Farm, East Lulworth, in 1837, to create the Lake (SY 861 839). His idea was to use it to test models of his racing yachts and to perfect the real thing; which is not that improbable as he was to make £3,000 in prize money and offered to design a brig for the Admiralty.

Joan Berkeley is cautious about this in *Lulworth and the Welds*: "Whether the Lake was made for that purpose I think is more doubtful: but I expect his little fort at the lakeside was made to hold the brig, and it remained there up to the last war when it was destroyed by souvenir hunters." The miniature fort was towards the north end of the wild western shore.

Landscape – the western end of the Isle of Purbeck where the countryside changes with the geology. Purbeck really ends where the sands and clays of the Great Heath give way to the gently rising masses of chalk on a wavy line from the sea at Arish Mell, East Lulworth, and northward. A belt of woods lies where the soils mix, and their names show how well popular etymology can describe the countryside – Long Coppice, Highwood (East Stoke parish), Monkton Bushes, Pepperclose Trees, Knap Coppice, Haremere Wood (Wool); Vicarage Coppice, Bramble Coppice, Eweyard Coppice, Kick Hill Coppice, Vary Clump, Ashy Drove, Duckpond Plantation, Kennel Wood, Lake Hill Plantation (Coombe Keynes); Gore Holmes, Seven Acre Withy Bed, Lodgewood, New Barn Plantation, Bowling Green Wood, Botany Wood, Broom's Plantation, Marl Plantation and Maiden Plantation (East Lulworth).

The south coast of Purbeck starts at a small bay, Arish Mell, at the centre of a much wider bay and where the sea has found a path inland by eroding the chalky gap between Bindon Hill on the west and Rings Hill rising sharply to the east. Sadly, Arish Mell is out of bounds, deep inside Royal Armoured Corps training ranges that were extended into Purbeck during the last war. Only a mile inland from Arish Mell, northward up the valley, stands amid trees the shapely grey mass of Lulworth Castle, impressive in silhouette, but with emptiness behind its walls. Built about 1609, and gutted by the fire of a single night in 1929, the castle is as dead as its history. Despite its appearance, Lulworth castle was simply a grand house, built to symbolise strength but without any military applications whatever.

East Lulworth's thatched cottages, lying on the edge of the castle grounds, are all that have survived the devastation of this locality. Elsewhere the people have gone and tanks and fire have reduced their homes to shells or less. The strange appeal of depopulation is to watch farmlands deteriorate into a wilderness restocked by wildlife. Above Tyneham the buzzard is there each day, soaring in widening circles; it is one of the few places in Dorset where I saw this then uncommon bird of prey maintain a countinuous presence through the sparse years until the present day when its numbers have increased dramatically.

On Whiteway Hill, whilst driving into Purbeck from Lulworth, it is often possible to count a dozen kestrels hovering in the wind above the overgrown escarpment and plunging frequently on to their plentiful prey. Roe deer, now common in woods throughout Dorset, have brought movement to Rook Grove and Tyneham Great Wood at the heart of a deserted parish. Wild land around Tyneham was created at the cost of people's homes, and yet it is possible to take some pleasure from the result. Natural habitats have recreated themselves in contrast to the diminution of such areas in countryside that is farmed properly.

A line of red flags extends from Charnel at the west end of Kimmeridge Bay and inland across the saddleback of the Purbeck Hills. It continues west of Creech Grange and over heathland to Holme Lane, the road from Stoborough that follows higher ground above the Frome meadows to East Stoke. The road, second of the road exits from Purbeck (the first drops into East Lulworth) is now tarred but it is remembered by older people as a rough track through fords and water splashes and between clumps of rhododendron, firs and hazel thickets.

Liberty — a gravestone in Kimmeridge churchyard records the tragedy of the shipwreck that took place beside Broad Bench, in the south-eastern extremity of Tyneham parish, and claimed a young boy in 1868. The schooner was temporarily beached on the notorious ledge but then slipped to her doom in deep water:

"ERECTED BY SCHOOLCHILDREN IN MEMORY OF JOHN DYER WHO WAS DROWNED WITH THE CREW OF THE *LIBERTY* OFF BROAD BENCH SEPT 26th 1868 AGED 12 YEARS."

Little Bindon — the Cistercian community of Bindon Abbey was founded by the sea, on the east side of Lulworth Cove (SY 831 798), in about 1150, and moved from there to an inland site at Wool in 1172.

The monks took the name Bindon with them and the ruins of the second Bindon Abbey stand beside the River Frome.

A Victorian map shows the "Site of Bindon Abbey," the original monastery, in the overgrown vale immediately north-east of the present Little Bindon but the Ordnance Survey no longer claims to know the site.

Little Bindon is the isolated chapel-cum-cottage in a wild gully at the east end of Lulworth Cove, with a hill separating it from the sea. It dates from about 1250, being taken over by rabbit-warreners and re-roofed around 1500, with brick dressings of the 1700s. Reset in the east wall of Little Bindon, below the gable, are two twelfth century carvings, from the original abbey. The west part of Little Bindon is now a cottage. For half a century it was the seaside retreat of eminent town planner Sir George Pepler [1882-1959].

Luckford Lake — overly impressive name for the only geographical feature on Purbeck's landward flank that is worthy of being called a boundary. It is a marshy tributary of the River Frome, which it joins at Stoke Common, East Stoke, set in the sloping fields north of Lulworth Park and trickling on across the heath beneath a canopy of sallow scrub.

The name "Lake" is also less expansive than it sounds, deriving merely from the Old English *lacu* "watercourse". It runs for little over a mile as a reasonable stream before it mingles unnoticed with a concourse of branches of the Frome at West Holme. Even its head is disputable as the stream is a collection of smaller waters from the ditches around ruined Whiteway Farm (below the west end of the Purbeck ridge); from the road drains of East Lulworth; and a trickle in Monkton Bushes, near the site of the sixteenth century Woodstreet Farm, demolished in the 1960s, which joins a ditch from Coombe Lots. The only impressive source is the overflow from The Lake, an expanse of water behind Home Farm between East Lulworth and Coombe Keynes (SY 862 839).

No one took Luckford Lake very seriously and it is only partially used for parish boundaries. This serves as an arbitrary border for Purbeck, though it fails to cut clearly from north to south as the hilly spine of Purbeck thrusts decisively upwards across its path.

Lulwind Cove — novelist Thomas Hardy's name for Lulworth Cove, which appears in *Desperate Remedies* [1871], *Far from the Madding Crowd* [1874], *A Tradition of 1804* [1882], and other works. From it Sergeant Frank Troy disappears, leaving his clothes on the beach, and is presumed drowned — giving Labour politician John Stonehouse the idea. The "Tradition" is the legend that Napoleon Bonaparte visited Lulworth Cove and decided, wisely, against invading here.

Lulworth Camp — seaside summer camps for volunteer soldiers had been held beside Lulworth Cove, usually in the area that is now the car-park, since Victorian times, but the military and their machines of the future arrived to stay in 1916. The War Office chose land at Lulworth for testing the world's first tanks. Weld-Blundell, the owner of Lulworth Castle, allowed the army to pitch its tents on the site of the present Lulworth Camp and the tank trials were carried out on the downland slopes of Bindon Hill between the Cove and Arish Mell.

The experimental unit with the first tanks was the Heavy Branch Machine Gun Corps, at Elveden in Suffolk. They moved to Dorset in 1916, as one of the first officers recalled in 1938:

"Wool, Bovington and Lulworth Cove were chosen for the headquarters of the Corps, and it was for camps near those delightful Dorset villages that we left Elveden late in November 1916. There we found a hive of activity, and recruits in plenty. Apparently infantry battalion commanders had been circularised and asked to recommend their 'most intelligent men, particularly those with some mechanical knowledge'.

"Needless to say, such a request produced the inevitable result, and we found that the new drafts consisted not infrequently of agricultural labourers and men with interesting crime sheets. But a year later I would not have exchanged one of these men for the most highly skilled mechanic in the country.

"At Wareham in 1918 there came back one faint echo of the heroic beginnings of the war, faint indeed as Roland's hour. A company of German prisoners and a company of Conscientious Objectors were put to work on the same fatigue. An hour later the German contingent arrived at Brigade Headquarters with a manifesto which read: 'We, the undersigned, being good men and true, who have borne with our English brothers the burdens of war, see no reason why we should be so disgraced as to have to work with these cowards.'

"The C.O. was amused and sympathetic. The Germans were given the afternoon off. They clicked heels happily, bowed with Teutonic dignity, and marched off with vast contented smiles."

Jack Lawley, the son of a range warden near Wareham, recalled for me his first sight of tanks in Dorset: "Then something new appeared on the heath around us, crawling about like huge tortoises. They were a new weapon of war, the tank. They would crawl up the hills, then dip their noses down and crawl down again."

After they were tested in the sparsely populated Dorset heaths, the world's first tanks rolled into battle on the Somme in 1916. "A pretty mechanical toy," was Kitchener's derisory comment. In this the war-lord summed up the general establishment reaction. The tank concept was pushed on to a reluctant War Office by Lieutenant-Colonel Ernest Swinton, serving not as a soldier but an official war correspondent, and who had written fiction under the pseudonym Backside-Forethought.

He had his invention rejected and then the idea was revived — this time in the unlikely surroundings of the Admiralty, where it had come to the notice of a former war correspondent, Winston Churchill. Never at a loss for a suitable name to disguise something that had no earthly relevance to his department, Churchill formed a "Landships Committee".

Nautical names were also found for the body of the machine, which was called the "hull", and to describe the thing itself which (after rejection of "cistern") became "tank". The army came back into the development programme which also received some timely royal patronage. King George V rode round the grounds of Lord Salisbury's Hatfield Park in a tank on 8 February 1916. To make the course a little more taxing, a ten foot trench had been dug and a four foot vertical obstacle prepared. The tank cleared both and impressed virtually everyone except Lord Kitchener. The King knew a good toy when he saw one and suggested that a large number in the army would be a great asset.

There were similar mixed reactions on the Front. When Major-General John Fuller saw his first tank he thought it was "a very graceful machine with beautiful lines" and that in use it would prove to be "an armoured mechanical horse". Of the first one hundred tanks, forty-nine went into action on 15 September 1916 and three from D-Company achieved the historically symbolic moment, which was witnessed from the air: "A tank is walking up the High Street of Flers with the British Army cheering behind."

The greatest success for the Tank Corps was on 19 August 1917. A decision had been taken that a string of pillboxes at St Julien had to be knocked out. Their walls were of reinforced concrete, more than three feet thick, and it was thought that the action would cost a thousand casualties. Instead the tanks went in first, followed by the infantry, under a smoke screen and without any preliminary bombardment. There were only two British deaths.

On 20 November 1917 a massed force of 350 tanks led by Brigadier-General Hugh Elles (right at the front in "Hilda" with the new Tank Corps banner flying from an ash stick) smashed through every line of trenches in the German front. It was the first time this had been achieved since the stalemate of trench warfare had begun. But the War Office estimated that such a breakthrough would take five months and £20,000,000 of ammunition. So no one followed through the breach.

There had to be a British cover-up. In this field the War Office often had more talent than they ever showed for fighting. They excelled themselves and produced a German hero who had halted the British advance. Never before had the British press been allowed to admit that there were any brave Germans, and yet here was a British witness saying with War Office blessing: "I came to a German field battery, every gun out of action except one. By this was lying a single German officer, quite dead. In front of him were five tanks which he had evidently suceeded in knocking out single-handed with his gun. A brave man." Also a mythical man. The whole story was invented.

It was a story that was put forward by the reactionaries for the rest of the war as a reason for abandoning the tank programme. Kitchener could no longer join in as he went down with the cruiser HMS *Hampshire*, which struck a mine in the North Sea. Tank tactics on the Front became over-restrained with a general policy of dispersal. By the end of the war the Germans had their own tanks and similar capabilities — the British line was broken whenever it was attacked by tanks. The French too had their tanks, though hardly a great contribution to the war effort, and they were attractively dismissed by Fuller as "a kind of kitchen range on tracks, unblushingly useless".

Tanks won the decisive battle of the Great War at Amiens on 8 August 1918, tearing a gap eleven miles wide through the German lines. The Kaiser said that evening: "It is very strange that our men cannot get used to tanks."

Nelson Thomson, a Purbeck quarryman retired at Langton Matravers, looked back to 1916, when he was a young shepherd at Lulworth for Alan Budden of Burngate Farm, as he talked to me in 1971:

"When they used to bring the tanks over from Bovington they used to shut us behind screens of hurdles or take us away so that we couldn't see them. They put an army control all along the roads and if anybody were within sight they used to put them off. It didn't make any difference because, when we were at Lulworth, the tanks was going along the road and firing there — and we was working there.

"What I used to have to do was to take the sheep down on to the range from five o'clock to nine o'clock in the morning and then they did start firing and I had to bring them back. Then at two o'clock I'd bring them down, some days, from two to three o'clock and then back again. And then from six o'clock to eight o'clock in the evening. One time there I can remember a military policeman came out and started chasing me: I had sheep and troops and everything all mixed up together out of the square, opposite from where their tanks was.

"When Lulworth Camp started it was all tents. They were sleeping under canvas. I can remember when the post office at Lulworth got hit with a shell. I don't know whether it was 1916 but there was an awful disturbance about it. Two shells went adrift somewhere — they said they ricocheted — and the post office and one of the houses got hit. The shells came from the tanks firing on the tank range at Lulworth."

St Andrew's Farm is a seventeenth century stone building that stands on the south edge of Lulworth Camp. The Thomson family moved into it just two months before the camp was established. They were the first of the two hundred families evicted to create the Government's Lulworth and East Holme Ranges across 7,500 acres of the finest scenery in Dorset. Eviction from St Andrew's was summarily enforced.

"We had very short notice to get out from there," Nelson remembered. "It was twelve o'clock midnight when we went away from that farm and went down to Coombe Keynes to a man named Mr Ford."

The tank brought the taste of advance to the stagnant warfare of the trenches. At home it brought defeat for the remote and insular peoples of the heath and hills of the Isle of Purbeck. In 1923 the War Department tired of its short lease over the land at Lulworth and applied to purchase the ranges. The first counter-attack against the Government was launched by the Daily Mail:

"The assault on Lulworth Cove is of all those vandalistic enterprises the most inexcusable. The intention is to establish a tank gunnery school there. The Daily Mail has always supported the cause of the tank against the 'bow and arrow' school at the War Office but we feel it is really preposterous to tell the British public that the only range suited for tanks is the most exquisitely beautiful stretch of the Wessex coast.

"A little investigation would prove that alternative sites can be found without any difficulty. If the War Office does not show itself reasonable the House of Commons will have to intervene to save the threatened area from its assailants."

S.P.B. Mais reported in the Daily Graphic:

"Lulworth Cove itself was originally included in the scheme. So little do the authorities know of the country that when it was pointed out to them that their western boundary extended to a point nine hundred feet west of a beauty spot at least as famous and often visited as Clovelly they said that 'west' was a misprint for 'east'.

"Judged from the point of view of fair play, it is questionable morality to hire by force a plot of ground which was already prospected as an eligible site for a seaside resort, turn it into wilderness, and then offer to buy it at wilderness rates. Not only is the area covered by the tanks turned from an artists' paradise into a scapegoats' hell, but the actual property of Lulworth Castle becomes valueless. They could not have hit upon a worse plot of ground from every point of view. More and more it is becoming difficult for the townsman in search of a holiday to find some place that is both beautiful and quiet. The stretch of coast between Swanage and Lulworth is absolutely unspoilt.

"No one is going to take a holiday in country where his way is constantly being barred owing to gun practice. Even now sentries demand passes before you are allowed over Bindon Hill. The danger area, by an amazing lack of foresight, includes the only fossil forest in Britain. Geologists and their pupils swarmed there. Now they will not be allowed even to see it.

"The fishermen of Lulworth depend largely for a living on their lobster pots: if they go in an easterly direction they have to be back before nine in the morning. They can no longer shelter in Mupe's [all the old fishermen called it 'Mupe's' rather than 'Mupe'] Bay when they are unable to make Lulworth."

One of the fishermen told Mais: "I fought for this bit of land and when I come home they try to starve me out of it." Weld-Blundell, lord of the manor of Lulworth, put the matter in stronger terms. "Even the Huns," he said with fury, "never did a thing like this."

Lulworth was then described in holiday propaganda as the "English Bay of Naples" and Mais seemed to have been the first person to make the pun about "collecting shells on a Dorset beach". Another kind of seashell: "It is not a game that I recommend to the many boy scouts and girl guides who are in camp nearby."

The Bournemouth Daily Echo reported on 30 November 1923 that not only was the future of the tank ranges under consideration but the War Office had been offered an alternative site on the other side of Lulworth Cove:

"Up to the present the War Office has made no announcements to relieve public suspense regarding its intentions for the future of Lulworth Cove.

"At this week's meeting of the Dorset County Council it was reported that no reply had been received to the protest of the council against the proposal to establish the Tank Gunnery School permanently at East Lulworth, and the only information available for the county authority was a statement that it is possible that the Army Council will not press the question of the purchase of the site but will continue to lease it.

"Lord Shaftesbury, the Lord Lieutenant of the County, could go no further than that, and the county council, equally with those people all over the country who wish to see our beauty spots preserved, must possess themselves in patience until the War Office thinks proper to give some indication of its attitude.

"The principal reason advanced for suggesting that the War Office may not purchase the site was, in the opinion of experts in the tank arm of the service, that the obvious line of development of the tank is in the direction of heavier armament and that with heavier guns being used the Lulworth range might prove inadequate. There is another point that is always worth bearing in mind — that the War Office has an alternative site offered them on the west side of the cove which would not interfere with the famous beauty spot."

The owner of Lulworth was joined by Thomas Hardy, Lord Shaftesbury, and Sir Alfred Fripp in his struggle against the War Office plan to acquire permanently 973 acres of land between Lulworth Cove and Arish Mell. The tanks won.

It was explained at the public inquiry into the 1923-24 proposals that there had been a clerical error in the setting out of the western boundary, caused by the insertion of the word "west" instead of "east" and it had therefore been "incorrectly assumed" by the press and public that Lulworth Cove itself was included. The boundary, the War Office continued, should have been specified as running to the east of the Cove, so that the range included Bindon Hill, and the firing would be infrequent and would consist mainly of light machine gun fire and "that as little inconvenience as possible would be caused to the public, the footpaths being allowed to be used on bank holidays,

Saturdays, Sundays and special occasions and that suitable approved bye-laws would be drawn up: and on these occasions opposition was withdrawn".

Exactly the same offering would deflate the 1967-76 Tyneham campaign. Whitehall simply pulls out the appropriate contingency plan for dealing with this sort of thing.

The second stage of War Office encroachment at Lulworth had been surreptitiously achieved, but the people had been promised a future without further war. By this time there was a scrap-heap of abandoned tanks on the Dorset heath to the north of Bovington Camp. In 1924 the poet Rudyard Kipling visited Bovington and complained that no one appreciated the historic significance of these tanks and as a result two were put into a shed the following year. They were "Little Willie", the world's first tank, and "Mother", the first fighting version. Each weighed twenty-eight tons. Others soon joined them.

Ironically, the first permanent buildings at both Lulworth Camp and Bovington were erected by enemy labour.

Eight houses at The Oval, close to the road junction at the north-east corner of Lulworth Camp (SY 836 816), were built by German prisoners of war in 1919. They were held in camp nearby and expressed relief to be working locally, having previously been marched daily to Bovington, a return journey of 12 miles, where they navvied to lay a branch railway line, build a bridge over the River Frome, and construct the factory-sized Central Workshops.

Royal visitors to Lulworth included King George V in April 1928. He followed in the footsteps of Amanullah Khan, Amir of Afghanistan, who had inspected a similar guard of honour on 20 March 1928 and was accomplishing a delicate balancing act between two great powers. He attempted to maintain his country's independence by signing treaties both with Great Britain and Soviet Russia.

Stage three of the expansion of the Lulworth ranges was carried out in 1939 when the coming of a new war removed the necessity for the niceties of public consultation. The range bye-laws were altered to include a larger danger area and the public was totally excluded from the area. The eastern boundary of the new range lay on the east side of Arish Mell (instead of the west) so that this little bay which had been so popular with picnickers and courting couples through the 1930s was forbidden territory for the first time. The tank collection at Bovington was broken up, literally, with a few being spared for use as stationary pillboxes.

Lulworth Camp and its Bindon Range were in the front-line during the Battle of Britain, with the Luftwaffe carrying out almost daily incursions through the summer of 1940 from their newly acquired bases on the Cherbourg peninsula. Air raid warnings were commonplace but the unexpected lone German aeroplane could be more dangerous.

One such opportunist sneaked towards the Camp a few minutes after All Clear had sounded on 23 August 1940. "Recruits had resumed their infantry training and were in the open as the aircraft approached", to quote from *Dorset at War*. "Sergeant J. Thompson shouted to them to get down and stay still. Eight bombs were dropped on the sportsfield, the ranges and at St Andrew's Farm. Two men were killed and seven injured, the latter including Sergeant Thompson who received severe leg wounds. He had been in the stores when he heard the aircraft approaching and but for his instant and brave response, when he put himself in the line of fire to warn the men, there would have been a greater number of csasualties."

Often the attackers were seen off by Spitfires from Warmwell, the RAF station midway between Lulworth and Dorchester, and Hurricanes from Exeter. They put down a number of enemy fighters and bombers — the latter usually returning from Bristol or other inland targets – with most of these coastal kills ending up in the sea. Some, however, crashed on or near the ranges, as did a couple of British fighters. Sergeant Snowdon of 213 Squadron lived to fight another day, bringing his crippled Hurricane down on to Lulworth's "C" Range in a successful emergency landing, having been hit by return fire whilst shooting down a Bf110.

In July 1941 the infantry brigade of General Bernard Montgomery's Third Division – veterans of the Dunkirk beaches – arrived at Lulworth from a camp at Abbotsbury, for conversion to armour. They would be equipped with Churchill tanks, trained at Lulworth and Bovington, and sailed to war in the Western Desert for what would be the famous victory over Rommel's Afrika Korps at El Alamein.

On 6 April, 1942, Lulworth Camp entertained the Prime Minister who came as the war-lord "to see my tanks". These were the new British machines that bore his name and he then inspected them on the side of Halcombe Vale, above Sea Vale Farm, East Lulworth. I have recorded the day in *Dorset at War*: "Ranks of Churchill tanks, the first to go into service, received their namesake's approval today in the Arish Mell valley on the Dorset coast. Prime Minister Winston Churchill had a full tour of the Gunnery Wing of the Armoured Fighting Vehicles School at Lulworth Camp. Some of the Churchill tanks have been refitted with six-pounder guns to give them much increased fire-power. The first production versions carry two-pounders."

The Workshop at the Camp was strafed on 14 December 1942, leaving it "an utter shambles" with Sergeant Jack Stevens fatally wounded and three other soldiers injured. Two German fighter-bombers had made a surprise attack, apoproaching from the east, across Tank Park, and then turning south-west to disappear over Lulworth Cove and out to sea.

As the war moved from its defensive years and into the offensive, the entire parish of Tyneham would be added to the ranges, along with extensive tracts of adjoining parishes. Tyneham's requisition, which took place just before Christmas in 1943, has its own entry.

The whole of south Dorset became an armed camp in the spring of 1944, with thousands of men and vehicles, most of them American. Lulworth and Tyneham were assigned to the Sherman tanks of the Second Armored Division, the backbone of V Corps of the First United States Army — codenamed Force O (for Omaha) and tasked to take what would be the bloodiest of the Normandy beach-heads in Operation Overlord. Theirs was the D-day armada that sailed from Portland and Weymouth and touched the shore of occupied France at 06.34 hours on 6 June 1944.

By 1947 there was a revival of interest in Lulworth and Tyneham's discarded tanks and those vintage specimens that had not been scrapped were gathered up again from the heaths and coast, where they had served as anti-invasion pillboxes, and put back into the museum at Bovington. "Little Willie" survived and so too did a reasonable spread of First World War tanks, including specimens of Mark I, IV, V, VIII and IX. There is also a miniature British tank, the 14-ton "Whippet" dated from 1916, and a "Peerless" armoured car built in 1917. The Second World War brought the museum a representative collection of foreign tanks as well.

New generation warfare became standard issue at Lulworth in 1960. Having cancelled Orange William, an anti-tank missile developed by Fairey Aviation, the War Office looked to the other wide of the globe and placed an order for 400 Malkara surface-to-surface weapons. These 222-lb wire-guided anti tank missiles, designed and manufactured by Australia's nationalised aircraft industry, were mounted in pairs on Humber Hornet scout cars that had been converted into rocket launchers.

Firing tests were carried out in Tyneham valley where the trees and scrub became draped with discarded wire. What was originally intended as an anti-tank weapon, with a 57-lb warhead, was found to perform equally well against static targets such as bridges and blockhouses. "Its accuracy is such that it can be guided through the openings in a concrete bunker or gun emplacement from more than a mile away," it was reported.

Malkara and its air-droppable Hornet armoured fighting vehicles became standard equipment for the British Army. Cyclops Squadron of the Second Royal Tank Regiment were fitted out with the Hornet/Malkara as a "go-anywhere" unit that could be airlifted by Argosy and other RAF transport planes.

Architecture at Lulworth Camp has evolved fitfully. Lines of huts from the Great War continued in use through changing times and designations, as the Gunnery Wing of the Armoured Fighting Vehicles School and then the Tactical School, next to brick-built high-storey multiple wing buildings of the 1930s. Almost incongruously, displacing 65-year-old huts, arose the space-age lines of the Maintenance Hangars of A-Vehicle complex, with a roof worthy of a huge hypermarket.

The ranges would see the destruction of 183 "over-quota" British Chieftain tanks, witnessed by Russian observers, as the Cold War was brought officially to a close [1993-94]. Colonel Sergei Slepnev remarked: "Two years ago I would never have thought this day possible but it is to be welcomed and I have been impressed by what I have seen here in Britain."

Lulworth Castle – romantic ruin at East Lulworth (SY 854 822), which has been a roofless shell since being gutted by fire after being opened to the public for a day in 1929. Its partial restoration and re-opening, by English

Heritage, is being carried out in stages over many years [1983-97].

Brick-built and faced with Portland stone, it gracefully symbolised strength but had no military application whatever. Thomas Howard, third Viscount Bindon, built the castle in 1608, having obtained a licence to "inclose and impark" a thousand acres at East Lulworth Park in 1605. It used to be thought by historians that his brother Henry had begun building the castle about 1590 (John Hutchins gives 1588) but in 1968 Miss Clare Talbot, archivist for Lord Salisbury, discovered a letter that Sir Robert Cecil, the Earl Salisbury, had received on 1 July 1608.

The letter was from Thomas Howard, third Viscount of Bindon, and contained a postscript telling Cecil he had given him the idea for building the new castle, which he had just started: "If the little pile in Lulworth Park shall prove pretty or worth the labour bestowed in the erecting of it, I will acknowledge as the truth is, that your Lordship's powerful speech to me at Bindon to have laid the first foundation of the pile in my mind, which ever since hath laboured for a speedy finishing for contentment of those, whose further liking of that place the care is taken."

The bulk of the work was carried out in 1609. Hutchins writes that the terrace round the house used to be called the "Cloisters", because it was paved with stone brought from the cloisters of Bindon Abbey — Wool's Bindon rather than Lulworth's Bindon.

Lulworth Castle attracted royalty on numerous occasions. James I hunted in the park in 1615. Charles II came in 1665 with his brother and son, who would contest the throne after his death, the Dukes of York and Monmouth. George III, the queen and three older princesses sailed in from Weymouth in 1789. A repeat visit took place in 1791 but the following year the sea prevented the *Juno* frigate from landing the royal party, with the exception of the Prince of Wales who was soaked in the process. The party returned by carriage a few days later. George III came back in 1792, making a total of four visits to Lulworth in the period 1789-92.

In June 1801 he was back again, at the Red Lion Inn at West Lulworth which had been immortalised by John O'Keeffe's play. The King was greeted by Matthew Randall, the son of the late landlord, "John Barleycorn".

Sir John Turbeville of Bere Regis garrisoned Lulworth Castle for the Royalists in 1643 though by the end of the year they had been replaced by Parliamentary foot soldiers under the command of Captain Thomas Hughes. They melted down some five tons of lead, stripped from country house plumbing, for use in the county, particularly the Corfe siege.

An interesting record survives from 1646 that shows the extent of bureaucracy and the concern to be seen to be above corruption — Hughes allowed himself to be in the position of receiving an order to hand over to the county treasurer three puncheons of spirit and a hogshead of white wine "washed ashore from the wrecks". Few commanders would be so careless with the gifts of nature and war.

Lulworth Castle was taken into guardianship by the Department of the Environment in the 1970s, giving the state the responsibility for its upkeep as an ancient monument, and it is now opened to the public. For its chapel, refer to the entry for "Lulworth Roman Catholic Chapel".

Lulworth Cove — classic textbook geology at West Lulworth (SY 826 798) where the sea has breached the hard limestone barrier of the outer cliffs and scooped out from the soft, coloured Wealden sands and clays behind a semi-landlocked bay of tennis-bat shape. The sea broke through at this point because of the valley cut by the small stream that now flows into the Cove beside the cluster of buildings. It made the initial opening through the ridge of

Purbeck/Portland rocks. On the inland side the cliffs are sheer and of chalk.

For almost a century the Cove received regular summertime visits from shallow-draught paddle steamers operating from Weymouth, Swanage and Bournemouth, which came right in to a landing stage of planking that extended from beside the outlet of the stream.

Shell fish used to be caught on some scale.

Mrs A. Moulder recorded a conversation with an elderly, weather-beaten Lulworth lady, in Dorset County Magazine in 1969: "Talking one day about fishing, she told me that since the coming of the Gunnery School lobster fishing had been severely restricted. Many years before, there had also been flourishing, profitable oyster beds. Oyster fishing was done on quite a large scale and an oyster pond was made on the west side of the Cove, where the fish were kept till wanted. She pointed to the outer wall of the pond, which could be seen at low water, though few people knew its origin."

The old lady was one of the last to remember that a fair was held on a broad stone jetty at Lulworth Cove each Easter Monday. This construction was washed away and the last fair stall was then pitched near the hotel. The memory of a forgotten fair at the water's edge; oyster shells that are now always empty; a smugglers' grappling-iron and tub that were discovered at Kimmeridge and hang from a wall in the museum at Dorchester — all these are reminders of the lives of old-time fishermen.

Lulworth meteor — sighted over Lulworth Castle at nine o'clock in the evening of the first Saturday of December in 1762 when a "sudden radiant light overspread the earth and sea, equal to the splendour of the noon-day sun."

The observer recorded that "looking directly over us we saw an appearance refulgent [dazzling] as the sun itself, in form straight as a line, about eight times the diameter of the full moon in length, the duration about a minute. Afterwards it altered its position and changed into a serpentine form, and seemed to terminate in smoke."

Lulworth Park Wall – encloses 550 acres of park and woodland at East Lulworth and is four miles in circumference. It was built by Thomas Weld and is said to have been completed in 1773, though the gate piers of the North Lodges have dated stones of 1785.

The park wall is of brown heathstone, known architecturally as carstone, repaired with brick. It rises in places from five to ten feet, with embattled parapets. Six round towers, six feet in diameter and fifteen feet high, are set at angles in its course.

Wareham Gate Lodge, a two storey building with parapets above an arched carriageway, has an 1808 date stone, but that merely records the rebuilding in its present position. It had been built in the seventeenth century "in front of the Castle" beside a garden and was taken down in 1753. The stones had lain in heaps for half a century when Thomas Weld decided to have it rebuilt beside the lane to Coombe Keynes (SY 858 828).

Lulworth Ranges – the Lulworth and East Holme tank gunnery range of the Ministry of Defence cover 7,501 acres and are effectively the western boundary of the Isle of Purbeck. They are spiked by only two public roads, one of which is often closed, and a network of coastal permissive footpaths which are open only when firing is not taking place. That is generally the case at weekends throughout the year, for the month of August, and over Christmas and the new year holiday.

The ranges include the lost village of Tyneham and have what is arguably the best bit of coastline in Dorset.

Footpath access was allowed much as now until 1939 when the public was totally excluded from the area. That year the range was extended to include Arish Mell Gap. In

December 1943 several square miles of western Purbeck were depopulated and added to the ranges, at a time when Dorset filled with American soldiers and the allied armies trained for the invasion of Europe. A public inquiry in 1947 consolidated the wartime gains.

In 1968 I founded the Tyneham Action Group in the first issue of Dorset County Magazine and entered a fight that ran for several years, with deputations to 10 Downing Street and the Ministry of Defence, before ending in 1975 with a typical British compromise. There was to be no return of land, but sufficient concessions restored public access to deflate any campaign. These Lulworth Range Walks provide a network of coastal footpaths through Tyneham village and across the coastal cliffs and hills between Lulworth and Kimmeridge.

Under the so-called Crichel Down rules, surplus government land can only be offered back to the former freehold owners or their descendants, and as the Tyneham population were tenants they could never have won a right of return inside the present system. In these circumstances it is a relief to conservationists that we never won, given that the area has become a wilderness, harbouring a reservoir of wildlife that has been breeding populations of peregrine falcon, hobby, buzzard and other birds of prey that were decimated by chemicals from civilian farmland. Military ecology is better than no ecology.

An equivalent piece of army landscape and ecology, though inland and on a far larger scale, is on the other side of the Atlantic at Suffield, Alberta. There a thousand square miles of virgin North American prairie is used as a mock battleground described by British officers as "one of the best training areas in the world". As with Tyneham, the Suffield ranges are a superb example of landscape conservation as there is "no other comparable stretch of prairie land in North America that remains so close to its original grassland state". Suffield also has its political campaign with ecologists urging that the land should be preserved in its wild state as a national park. In both cases the army has allowed nature to recreate an enriched wild environment which contrasts with the restrained uniformity of man's surrounding farmlands.

Lulworth Roman Catholic Chapel — the Palladian-style "great chapel" in the Park (SY 853 823) at Lulworth Castle has a notable place in ecclesiastical history, as it was the first purpose-built Catholic church to be built in England since the Reformation. The Gordon Riots had taken place in 1780 but Catholics were given back partial freedom by the Relief Act of 1778.

Permission for the Lulworth building was granted by the King, George III, though the Weld family tradition is that he stipulated it should look more like a mausoleum or temple than a church. The architect was John Tasker and work started in December 1785 with the "quarrying stone at Bindon Warren, taking down stone at Bindon Abbey", and "Worbarrow Stone for the plinth" or foundations.

The cut stone for the main building was brought by sea from Portland, via the Cove and Worbarrow, and the altar was put in place in 1787. Bodies and monuments were brought from East Lulworth parish church to give validity to the pretence that the building was a mausoleum. The series begins with Mary Weld [died 1650] and Sir John Weld [died 1674].

There is no surviving record of the consecration of the church, which must have been regarded as a matter private to Catholics, but the church assumed a higher profile in 1790 when it was used to consecrate the American prelate John Carroll as Bishop of Baltimore, and Bishops Douglas and Gibson of London and northern England.

Thomas Weld [1750-1810], "the handsomest small man in England", consistently refused to join the Catholic Committee, which lobbied to remove the last legal restrictions on the faith, but reluctantly signed a

"Declaration and Protestation by the Catholics of England". He considered the campaign might harden Protestant attitudes but saw Chief Minister Pitt in London to take exception to a proposed legal description of "Protesting Catholic Dissenters" and succeeded in removing this from the second Catholic Relief Act which received the royal assent on 10 June 1791.

Joan Berkeley points out in *Lulworth and the Welds* that Thomas Weld was a realist who accepted that no further major amelioration of the law would be possible for at least a generation, as George III, his friend, was adamant that the coronation oath prevented him from consenting to further legal relaxations.

Lulworth Skipper – a species of butterfly new to Britain when it was first caught above Durdle Door, west Lulworth, on 15 August 1832. The specimen was taken by the eminent entomologist J.C. Dale [1791-1872] of Glanvilles Wootton, near Sherborne, who realised that the little khaki creatures, which were flitting about the downland in some numbers around the general area of Lulworth Cove, were something quite unusual.

He was lucky in his choice of high summer for a trip to the seaside because they are on the wing only for a period of about six weeks from mid-July to late August.

Thymelicus acteon became known as the Lulworth Skipper. Its British records are almost entirely restricted to the coast from the eastern side of Lyme Bay along to Swanage. The larvae are grass feeders but the butterflies are attracted to the purple flowers of the thistle, rest-harrow and marjoram. Dale's original first specimens are preserved with his collections at Oxford.

Lutton – ruined farmstead in the parish of Steeple, lying a kilometre west of the village (SY 901 809) and incorporated into the Lulworth Ranges [1943]. The last occupant was farmer Albert Ernest Cranton. Beside the remains of his home are the traces of a more extensive mediaeval settlement. Its footings rise as dry islands in an otherwise boggy field in a collection of minor earthworks that spread across five acres.

Maiden's Grave Gate — on the site of an ancient crossroads, inside the Lulworth Ranges, at the boundary between Tyneham and Steeple parishes (SY 892 814) with a windswept old oak known as the Coffin Tree. That was so called because of the shapes of two small coffins, a few inches across, cut into the trunk. The second appears to have been carved as the first became obliterated.

The names of the gate and the tree, together with the symbols, preserve the memory of a girl who killed herself probably in the late eighteenth century and was deprived of Christian burial: she was deposited instead, as law and custom demanded, at night by the highway by a crossroads, as far as possible from the village church — preferably, as here, on the parish boundary — and with a stake driven through her heart to prevent the appearance of a ghost. But who she was we shall probably never know.

The Examiner newspaper reported on Christmas Day in 1814 that after the death of a nobleman, Lord French, an inquest was being held on the body and a verdict of insanity returned. The paper commented: "Had the unhappy man been in the humble instead of the elevated walk of life, he would most likely have been deemed 'sane', and have been barbarously buried in the highway with a stake through his body! Any verdict however may be deemed better than one which leads to results at once so stupid in itself, so afflicting to relatives, and so disgusting to everybody."

Man o' War Cove — the inner corner of St Oswald's Bay, on the opposite side of the Durdle Door promontory, named from the Man o' War rock which divides it offshore from the main bay (SY 809 802). The rock could have been named for its shape but may well have also claimed a warship amongst its inevitable tally of shipwrecks.

These cliffs feature as Dagger's Grave, inspired by the actual Daggers Gate a kilometre north-west, in Thomas Hardy's smuggling tale *The Distracted Preacher* [1879]. That gate was probably named for someone who had the surname Dagger.

Milestone – an arm of the Wareham Turnpike Trust [1765–1876] extended for a mile beyond Holme Bridge, in the direction of East Lulworth. This was on the line of the present B3070 and the end – or rather the beginning – of the Trust's responsibilities was marked by a milestone in the middle of the unfenced heath.

It stood on the west side of the road on the eastern slope of Five Barrow Hill, in the parish of Tyneham (SY 877 840), and was inscribed "LONDON 117, LULWORTH 2".

Monastery Farm – a derelict farmhouse on the Lulworth Ranges, in the Arish Mell valley, immediately below the western end of the Purbeck Hills at East Lulworth (SY 861 810) had a remarkable history from 1796 until 1817.

The ruined Abbey of Our Lady and Saint Susan, otherwise known at Monastery Farm, was the first Cistercian monastery to be established in the British Empire since the Reformation, by a group of monks led by Pere Jean-Baptiste who left La Trappe after the suppression of the French religious houses by the national assembly in 1790.

Thomas Weld, the head of one of Britain's oldest Catholic families, offered them a refuge on his lands at Lulworth. This was completed in March 1796. The monks gave thanks for their asylum and undertook to drink nothing but water in the future. Alan E. Horton tells in issue 93 of Dorset County Magazine how the events of the time compromised traditional British tolerance:

"Yet these were troubled times and being a French community, even with English recruits, they were constantly under suspicion of harbouring spies. In 1803 a report was even spread that Jerome Napoleon was hidden there! Then a traitor among them renounced his religion and drew up a list of wild accusations against them. The Prime Minister, Lord Sidmouth, summoned Dom Antony to London to answer the charges. An enquiry followed and all the charges proved false but, in spite of this and the high compliment paid by the Premier to the Abbot's honour and integrity, the force of public opinion caused an order to be made requiring that no subject of the British crown should be admitted to the novitiate."

For giving refuge to the Trappists, Thomas Weld [1750-1810] became the target of pamphleteers, with the appearance in London in 1801 of "The Canonization of Thomas —— Esq who has lately erected at East L——h, Dorset, a monastery, and therein established a body of Monks. The Stanzas by Sternhold and Hopkins, Poets Laureate to the Monastery: The Notes by Addison, Abp. Tillotson, Hume, Duigenan, Rennell, Abp. Newton, Voltaire, Bp. Sherlock, and Judge Blackstone." Weld took the attacks and accepted them philosophically – "one must accept these squibs" – and duly listed the purchase of the pamphlet in his ledger: "To my Canonization 2s.6d."

The Napoleonic invasion and spy scares reached a peak in 1803 and rumours inevitably spread concerning the emigré monks on the Lulworth coast. Thomas Weld issued the following notice, with a reward for tracking down the source of the stories:

"Having been industriously circulated, in the neighbourhood of Lulworth Castle, in the County of Dorset, that Jerome Bonaparte was concealed in the said Castle, or in a house near that place, belonging to Thomas Weld, Esq., which is inhabited by some emigrant monks of the order of La Trappe, and that arms and ammunition were deposited there, which report, however difficult and impossible to be credited by well-informed persons, has nevertheless gained belief among many of the illiterate common people, we, the undersigned Magistrates of the County of Dorset, anxious to quiet the minds of such persons as may have given credit to the above report, and to satisfy them that it is unfounded as it is wicked and foolish, have examined every part of the Castle and house above mentioned, and, as might be expected, have not found any Arms and Ammunition concealed there, or any person whose appearance could give rise to the story; and we take this opportunity of cautioning all such persons against being in future misled by any reports of a similar nature, which can only be propagated by ill-disposed designing persons, to gratify their own private malice by creating unjust suspicions against a truly worthy and respectable character, who is well-known to the whole County of Dorset for his loyalty and attachment to his King and country. We were accompanied on our search by the Constable, Churchwarden, and Overseer of the Poor of the Parish of East Lulworth.

LIONEL DAMER.
JAMES FRAMPTON.
ROBERT WOODMAN, Constable.
ROBERT SEYMOUR, Churchwarden.
GEORGE DAGWORTHY, Overseer.

Lulworth Castle, 14 August, 1803

The said Thomas Weld hereby offers a reward of ONE HUNDRED POUNDS, to be paid by Mr Mansfield, Attorney-at-Law, DORCHESTER, to the person or persons discovering the propagator of the above Report, on his or her conviction."

A vivid if desolate account survives of the rigours of life in the Trappist community at Monastery Farm. *A Pilgrimage to the Monastery of La Trappe* is one of the rarest of Dorset books. It was published anonymously, being printed at Havant for "private circulation" in 1815.

It says that after fleeing from France the monks had eventually been given sanctuary in Russia. But they refused to occupy their allotted lands when they heard that the property had been seized from the peasants by the state. The Tsar was infuriated at this rejection of his generosity and had the monks deported to Hamburg.

Thomas Weld of Lulworth Castle found them the coastal valley beneath Flower's Barrow hillfort and erected a monastery "of a quadrangular shape, with a schilling on the inside, forming the cloisters; and in the area a depository for the dead. We observed seven graves [spring, 1813], to some of which were added a wooden cross, either at the head or feet. The living may be said to reside with the dead; and that they may be continually reminded of their mortal state, a grave is always left open for the reception of the next that dies; and we were told, that each individual prayed sincerely that he himself might soon become the occupier." Burials were undertaken without ceremony.

A handwritten note, inserted into a copy of this work, is less than admiring of the strict rules: "The Superior, the Law Agent, and the Porter were alone dispensed from the extreme vigour of the law of silence. The other members of the community were allowed one last word to their fellow creatures, but that in the agony of death and to confess their past transgressions. A wretch extended on an iron couch excited all his commiseration, for though he was writhing with pain, he was not deemed sufficiently ill to be allowed to explain the symptoms of his malady to the medical brother who consequently prescribed as it is natural to presume with unaided conjectural science. In a word, everything in and connected with the establishment seemed revolting to the mind of a civilised being, the substitution of devotional practices to the true maxims of our holy religion."

Visitors were received at the porter's lodge, on the west side of the farm. The porter wore a long brown robe of coarse cloth, and a cowl over his head, with a leather girdle around his waist from which the keys dangled. He did speak, in a whisper, but only to ask everyone to be silent. The eyes and noses only of the other monks were visible as they went "gliding along intent on meditation".

Their chapel was elegantly neat but not highly decorated, with a turret and dome at the centre. The high altar had a crucifix and, under a tabernacle, terracotta or wooden panel reliefs of the Virgin and Child. Each monk had his own named stall. There had been in all eighty-six of them at Lulworth.

The cells where the monks slept had only wooden beds with one blanket and a coarse rug — these compartments ranged together "like so many caves of death".

The surrounding farm, "with the assistance of a carter and his boy" was sufficient to provide the monks with their restricted diet — on which they all looked well — and surplus produce was sent to Poole. Waking time began at one a.m. throughout the year and devotions in the chapel continued for eight hours. Manual labour, with prayer breaks, followed till the afternoon. Their one meal of the day, solely of vegetables, was at 1.30, and reading, meditation and prayers took up the rest of the day until they went to bed at 8 p.m.

No one drank anything but water. These ascetics had little left to give up, but when they left France they had vowed that if they could find permanent asylum somewhere in Europe they would show their thanks by drinking nothing but water in the future. Their reward was offered in another world, beyond Heaven's gate: "Far from the world's deceiving path we fly. To find a passage to . . . Eternity."

As the anonymous author remarked, the people of Dorset had “no fear that the silent order of La Trappe will ever extend its influence into the neighbouring villages”.

The community was raised to the status of an abbey in 1813, and its first Abbot – Dom Antony – was a Sorbonne litterateur and doctor, Charles Saulnier de Beauregarde. But the ban on its recruitment of Britons meant that the abbey could have no future. Dom Antony returned to France, and arranged for the community to take over the Cistercian monastery of Melleray, one of only two still intact, and a French frigate, *La Revange*, was sent to collect them in July 1817. Their twenty-five dead were taken to Leicester for reburial at Mount St Bernard's Abbey in 1952, after the farm was permanently incorporated in the tank firing ranges. Monastery Farm lies out-of-bounds on the eastern side of the Arish Mell valley but it can be seen from above, from the rampart of Flower's Barrow hill-fort when the army's network is open, which is most weekends.

Mupe Bay, Rocks and Smugglers Cave – signposted diversion from the coastal path inside the Lulworth Ranges (SY 842 797). When the range walks are open there is unrestricted access to Mupe beach, which tends to be out of the prevailing wind as it faces east. The cliffs are multi-coloured sands, with triangular rocks jutting up like shark's teeth in a line offshore.

To the right, beyond the first line of Mupe Rocks, you come to a second cove. At the far end lies the Smugglers Cave, as the map now calls it though it was formerly known as Bacon Hole.

It is remarkable as it has a false-wall, about eight feet high, built across its back end. This wall encloses a chamber about fifteen feet wide by ten feet deep. There are the remains of a door, though this could have been concealed by rocks. The main cave is forty feet deep and about twenty-five feet wide.

On the clifftop above the Smugglers Cave is the ruin of a small stone building, about eight feet square, which had its doorway facing the cliff edge and the open sea. A little further to the west is a wartime pillbox with crinkle-cut walls, resulting from its concrete being poured into corrugated shuttering.

Napoleon's reputed visit — there is a firm tradition that the French ruler Napoleon Bonaparte [1769-1821] landed in Lulworth Cove during the period of invasion scares at the start of the nineteenth century. In the 1930s the Women's Institute at Lulworth noted their generally accepted version of the legend for the book *Dorset Up along and Down along*. The "Emperor" was seen by a young farmer's wife who spoke French and heard him sigh "Impossible" as he folded his charts and walked back towards his ship. His famous cocked hat was by no means unique to the Emperor; but on the other hand his features had been popularly available as caricatures and cartoons. So the woman might have been able to identify him.

The story is relayed with a positivism rarely heard with oral tradition: "The whole incident was watched and the conversation overheard by a local farmer's wife who had learnt French as a young girl so that she might help her father (a china merchant) in his business. This lady was born in 1874, and lived to be 104, and was alive when the West Lulworth contributor first heard the story."

The most likely year for this visit would have been 1804 when Napoleon was emperor and personally supervising the invasion fleet being assembled at embarkation points along the eastern end of the Channel. For eighty days he was based at Pont-de-Briques, a chateau near Boulogne, and though this period is intensely documented there are a few days when Napoleon's movements are unknown.

He could have slipped across to England but the fact is that despite the succession of alarms in Dorset it was Caesar's Coast — as the War Office called Kent in the summer of 1940 — that was the objective of the Grande Armée. That choice would have been enforced by the tides, as David Cooper points out in issue ten of Dorset County Magazine: "The ebb out of Boulogne would take the fleet to the west but the flood tide on the English coast would then bring it back eastwards." It would also be pushed up-Channel by the prevailing south-westerly winds.

There was not, then, any prospect of invading Lulworth from Boulogne. Nearer and easier were the sandy beaches of Poole Bay, not that the Grande Armée was in a position for visiting them either. Nor was the French intelligence such that it needed to ascertain landing conditions on the Dorset coast; information about the English coast and its defences had been collected for centuries, and as Cooper says Napoleon approved "the sending of spies to England and of corsairs to capture English peasants and fishermen for interrogation".

Despite that I do feel it was completely in character for Napoleon to have taken a day off for the express purpose of enjoying a few steps on English soil, and Dorset may have been considered much less risky than the actual piece of coast that was the target for the two thousand craft that were being prepared to carry a hundred thousand men. There might well have been a plan for a diversionary attack to draw the English fleet down-Channel in the direction of Dorset.

Napoleon was keeping up the pressure from Brest for this express purpose, and it had an effect as George III showed in June 1804 when he told the Duke of York: "I cannot deny that I am rather hurt there is any objection made to forming so large an Army of Reserves in Dorsetshire where, or in Cornwall, I think an attack more likely than in Essex, Kent or Sussex." When the King later approved the country's anti-invasion precautions and garrisons he asked for more troops to be provided in Dorset

— "for Dorset is one of the most vulnerable parts of the kingdom".

Newlands Farm — on the downs a mile west of West Lulworth (SY 811 811), was the principal holiday haunt of the promiscuous philosopher and mathematician Bertrand Russell [1872-1970]. The rather bland eighteenth century building has rendered walls and its beauty is in the setting into which it looks, particularly the view of the whole length of Bindon Hill was the external attraction of Russell's favourite bedroom, on the east side of the farmhouse.

There he had all the major lovers of his life, from 1916 until the mid-30s, including Lady Ottoline Morrell, Colette O'Neil (Lady Constance Malleson), Dora Black, Katherine Mansfield, Vivien Eliot (first wife of T.S. Eliot), Dorothy Wrinch, and Patricia ("Peter") Spence. Several of them, and members of their various cliques, went for nude bathes in Lulworth Cove, and otherwise scandalised the village with activities that are hinted at in the novel which Colette O'Neil wrote around their relationship.

Russell became Earl Russell on his brother's death in 1931. He was a prolific writer on mathematical and philosophical subjects, branching out with books on *Marriage and Morals* and *In Praise of Idleness*, but it was for pacifism that he would be famous in old age. As the leading figure in the anti-nuclear Committee of One Hundred he was frequently imprisoned during the civil disobedience campaigns of the 1960s.

Ocean Seat—favourite picnic place and arbour of the Bond family from the former Tyneham House, overlooking Brandy Bay from the grassy cliffside 400 yards south of their home (SY 889 798). Now inside the Lulworth Ranges but accessible once again on the main coast path, when it is open, between Gad Cliff and Tyneham Cap.

As well as the stone seat there was an adjoining shelter, sometimes used as a coastal lookout, ruins of which can be traced.

O'Keeffe – Irish playwright **John O'Keeffe** [1747-1833] visited West Lulworth in 1791 and stayed at the Red Lion, the house just north of the war memorial which is now known as Churchfields. It also served for a time as the toll-gate. The innkeeper was William Randall [1728-94] with his wife Ann, who had five daughters and one son. Randall was to provide O'Keeffe with his central character John Barleycorn for the farce *The London Hermit, or Rambles in Dorsetshire, A Comedy in Three Acts, as performed with Universal Applause at the Theatre Royal, Haymarket*, to quote its first edition title page of 1793. It is dedicated to Rev John Ball of Winfrith.

O'Keeffe remembered William Randall in his *Recollections*, published in 1826:

"The greatest original in person, manner and dress ever seen. He was tall, thin and bony with a long shallow face and staring eyes. His dress usually a white flannel coat, scarlet waistcoat with brass buttons, brown corduroy breeched, brown thread stockings and thick solid shoes with iron buckles. Besides performing the duties of innkeeper to perfection he was a man of all trades. He farmed the land, mended the doors and windows and repaired roofs. He painted names on the stern of the local fishing boats charging a penny a letter. He was adept at cobbling shoes and had painted the 'Red Lion' on his own sign board. To amuse himself he strummed a bass viol, and Sundays sang in the Church choir. If need arose, he was always ready to act as courier carrying messages to Poole, Blandford or Dorchester. When speaking, he gesticulated wildly, swinging his arms and head about, and continually stammering over the many long and fine sounding words with which he attempted to embellish his speech."

Paul Randall wrote about the characterisation in the play of his ancestor and his family in issue seventy-five of Dorset County Magazine:

"The comedy is set in and around the Red Lion which is specifically mentioned, as is Lulworth in the script. William Randall figures under the name of John Barleycorn and his daughter, 'Kitty', is a principal character. She is described as a girl educated beyond her station which may well have been near the truth.

"The play is somewhat dated but the minor characters are delightful. The Boots, 'John Grum', is shown as a real country bumpkin whose only lines consist of 'Ah' or 'Um'. Apparently on the first night his appearance was so droll and the applause was so great that he needed to say nothing.

"One wonders if 'John Barleycorn' was sufficiently interested in his representation to persuade his family to see the play in town on the boards of the Haymarket Theatre but William's first visit to London was such that he probably preferred to stay at home."

In his *Recollections* O'Keeffe recalled his morning dips in Lulworth Cove and how he had asked a fisherman why he did not bathe. He was told: "Not I, master, I keep out of the water as much as I can, and I am sure I cannot see why, for my part, you London folks come down here at a vast expense, to souse and sop yourself in salt water."

Old Bond Street – cottages beside Grange Road, half a mile north of Creech Grange (SY 917 829), nicknamed as an allusion to New Bond Street in London which was being laid out [1830] by Sir Thomas Bond who had connections with the nebulous western Purbeck landowning family.

Pennie – author and aesthete **John Fitzgerald Pennie** [1782-1848] was East Lulworth's child progidy. He was born at the Vicarage, where his parents seem to have been in domestic service, and though self-taught he had by the age of fifteen produced a tragedy, *The Unhappy Shepherdess*, and a neighbour, Captain Hay Forbes, had sufficient confidence in Pennie to arrange him an interview with the manager of the Covent Garden Theatre.

He told him to return to Dorset and write another play and Pennie was to find his way into a travelling band of players. His first attempt at producing his own comedy, at Shaftesbury in 1810, was a dismal failure and left him in poverty. A benefit performance of his own *Gonzanga* was given at Chepstow in 1814 and little more attention was given to him until *Ethelwolf*, or the *Danish Pirates* was put on in Weymouth in 1827.

Pennie published his first epic, *The Royal Minstrel* in 1817 and started a school at Lulworth but it had closed by 1828 when he moved to Keysworth Cottage, north of Wareham. His life's achievement dated from his time at Lulworth; the publication in 1827, under the name Sylvaticus, of *The Tale of a Modern Genius*, his account of an aesthete's bitter struggle against abuse and neglect, with descriptions of Purbeck.

From Keysworth he moved to Stoborough Heath where friends had helped him build a cottage which he called *Rogvald* after his second epic. The rest of his life was marred by debt, on behalf of his family, and he died within a couple of days of his wife in 1848. They were buried at East Lulworth.

Pepler — town planner **Sir George Lionel Pepler** [1882-1959] had Little Bindon, West Lulworth, as his secluded wild retreat for half a century. There his great passion was for a good bonfire as he held back the acres of bramble bushes in what was virtually his own private valley on the eastern side of Lulworth Cove.

Nationally, from 49 Rivermead Court, Hurlingham, London SW6, he was the creator of the urban jungle that sprawls across great tracts of south-east England.

He laid out large estates and mapped the forerunner of the motorway system, the arterial roads that resulted from a series of conferences he organised [1914].

Between the wars he took on slums and aviation, as a member of the Unhealthy Areas Committee [1921] and the Aerodromes Advisory Board [1934]. During this time he was Chief Town Planning Inspector for the Ministry of Health [1919-41]. He was then chairman of the Inter-Allied Committee for Physical Planning and Reconstruction [1942-45] and Chief Technical Adviser to the Ministry of Town and Country Planning [1943-46], and was rewarded with a knighthood [1948].

He then helped organise the Festival of Britain [1951] and the expansion of Singapore [1950-54], and was particularly pleased to receive the first gold medal awarded by the Town Planning Institute [1953].

Pepler's Point – promontory on the east side of the entrance to Lulworth Cove (SY 828 796), named for Sir George Lionel Pepler who for fifty years rented Little Bindon, in the valley to the north-east, as his holiday and retirement cottage.

On the exposed headland a stone seat is his memorial, with plenty of words to tell us that he "loved the land of England . . . and Dorset best of all" but none reveal that he was Britain's leading town planner. I wonder why.

Phantom Roman Army – the spectre said to haunt the western end of the Purbeck Hills, inside what are now the Lulworth Ranges.

The momentous sighting, the one that caused national consternation, was in December 1678 when Captain John Lawrence of Creech Grange, Steeple, in the company of his brother and four clay-cutters, were astonished to see a hostile army of massive proportions marching along the top of the ridge above Tyneham, from Flower's Barrow. The captain and his party fled to Wareham to raise the alarm and send warning to London, where Lawrence deposed the particulars on oath.

Lawrence described a force of several thousand armed men, and in preparation to meet them three hundred militia were hastily marshalled in Wareham. The South Bridge was barricaded. Scouts were dispatched to reconnoitre the coast but they found no trace of the hostile force, nor any evidence of a mass movement of men.

The phantom army, as it has come to be known, is held to presage a war; though 1678 was seven years from the Duke of Monmouth's rebellion and a decade away from William of Orange dethroning the Stuart monarchy.

Pondfield Cove — tiny bay, only 100 yards across, between Worbarrow Tout and Gold Down (SY 871 796). Inside the Lulworth Ranges but accessible, from Tyneham village or via the coastal path, when the Range Walks are open.

Though stony it is perfectly sheltered on both sides, west and east, and is exposed only to the southerly winds. The path into it, on the north side, is between concrete dragon's teeth anti-tank obstacles [from 1940].

After the war, Pondfield Cove was selected [1946-47] by Royal Engineer bomb disposal units for the detonation of warheads and shells that defied deactivation. The cove was screened from the rest of the Lulworth Ranges by Worbarrow Tout and Gad Cliff, and miles from the nearest occupied buildings.

Some of the explosions were massive, in order to trigger difficult ordnance, such as armour-piercing shells that had been delivered from locations as far away as Dover.

Povington — mile-long hamlet formerly strung out along the lane from East Lulworth to West Creech, from west to east across the central part of Tyneham parish (SY 880 820). Incorporated in the Lulworth Ranges [1943] and now almost entirely destroyed, with no public access. It lay between the Purbeck Hills and the Great Heath.

Parts may be glimpsed from Povington Hill (SY 888 811), but it is difficult to spot the few surviving walls of a series of little clusters of cob and stone walled farmsteads, cottages and barns that were mainly thatched. They date in the main from the seventeenth and eighteen centuries but the community had a far longer history.

The likelihood is that four Saxon demesne farms collectively make up the Domesday Book entry for Povington [1086]. Some of the little fields date back long before the Parliamentary enclosures and have that sort of antiquity. Povington manor was given by a Norman baron, Robert Fitzgerald, to the Abbey of Bec in Normandy. It was confiscated by Henry V in his dissolution of alien priories and presented to Eton College. Then it came into state hands through a land exchange and was given by Edward VI to the Duke of Somerset, whose name survives on a piece of land that has reverted to heath at Earl's Kitchen. After Somerset's attainder, Queen Elizabeth passed it to Edward, Earl of Hertford, who extinguished the manor by selling the demesnes and copyholds to the tenants.

Buildings at Povington included Whiteway Farm, Farwell's Cottage, Jiggiting Corner, Povington Farm, and Searley's Holdings.

Povington Hill — Iron Age Celtic field system, of both regular and irregular shapes, across twenty-five acres on the top of the Purbeck Hills, inside the Lulworth Ranges to the north-east of Tyneham village (SY 888 812).

Povington stone circle — destroyed in the nineteenth century, but stood below the northern shoulder of the Purbeck hills, inside the Lulworth Ranges to the north of Tyneham (SY 867 818). It is recorded by Charles Warne in his *Ancient Dorset* [1872] "within living memory between East Lulworth and Povington, but not a vestige of it remains". His informant, J.F. Pennie, said the stones were taken away by a farmer named Bower and used by him for gateposts and a bridge over a stream.

No later information has been forthcoming, but on examination of maps I was surprised to find at a point midway between East Lulworth and Whiteway the name of Rempstone Gate. It is where the old county road crosses the East Lulworth and Tyneham parish boundary.

The Rempstone Gate area has no less than ten round barrows within a short distance and nearby, beside the present road to Whiteway Hill, is Bower's Coppice, preserving the name of the farmer's family. The only other occurrence of the name Rempstone in Purbeck is near Corfe Castle, at a place which also has a Bronze Age stone circle.

The fact that both placenames are connected with stone circles is sufficient to discredit the accepted but unproven view that Rempstone at Corfe took its name not from the stones but a family that settled in Purbeck. Any notion that the name was transferred from Rempstone to Povington by one of Dorset's fanciful antiquaries can be discounted as Rempstone Gate was so called during the nineteenth century, if not earlier, and the circle at Rempstone itself was not even noted by archaeologists until 1908.

Randall — innkeeper **William Randall** [1728-94] of the Red Lion, now known as Churchfields, in West Lulworth, provided playwright John O'Keeffe with "the greatest original in person, manner and dress ever seen". Randall became John Barleycorn, the central character in *The London Hermit, or Rambles in Dorsetshire* [1793]. (See O'Keeffe's entry for details of the play.)

Rings Hill — descriptive local name for the slopes below Flower's Barrow hill-fort, at the western end of the Purbeck Hills (SY 684 806). Flower's Barrow is much the older name, deriving from *Flouresberi* [1381], but Rings Hill has been in use for some time and appears in the parish tithe assessments [1841].

Royal visits – Lulworth Castle attracted princes and kings for four centuries, with the monarch list including James I, Charles II (as Duke of York), George III, George IV (when Prince of Wales), deposed King Charles X of France, and Edward VII.

George III also called at Churchfields, then the Red Lion, to visit Matthew Randall [1802]. He was the son of William "John Barleycorn" Randall [1728-94], who had been immortalised in John O'Keeffe's farce *The London Hermit, or Rambles in Dorsetshire* [1793].

Twentieth century royal visitors have generally been to Lulworth Camp, starting with King George V [April 1928] who followed Amanullah Khan, Amir of Afghanistan [20 March 1928], who was playing power politics in the mountains between the British and Russian empires.

Rubens – Flemish artist **Peter Paul Rubens** [1577-1640] is represented in at least one Dorset collection. In 1988, Colonel Sir Joseph Weld of Lulworth heard from Dr Michael Jeffe of the Fitzwilliam Museum, Cambridge, that he had a Rubens in his collection.

The previously unattributed drawing of *The Circumcision* had been bought in Genoa by Richard Houlditch. On his death in 1760, it was sold to William Roscoe. At the dispersal of his collection in 1816 the buyer was Charles Robert Blundell of Ince, near Liverpool, whose family later intermarried with the Welds.

St Andrew's Farm – seventeenth century house, barn and cottage within the confines of Lulworth Camp (SY 837 811). The use of the saint's name perpetuates a connection with a vanished chapel. Thomas Howard, third Viscount Bindon, built a "capital" chapel in this western part of East Lulworth parish. Joan Berkeley writes in *Lulworth and the*

Welds: "No doubt he is there still, but the exact site of the chapel and tomb is unknown."

The spot given on the large scale Ordnance Survey maps, as the site of St Andrew's Chapel, is just west of the closest army building on the north side of the farm. The farm itself is stated to be "on site of Manor House".

Shipwrecks – the rocky coastline from Lulworth to Swanage, exposed to south-westerly gales, has a catalogue of wreck and rescue to rival Portland's Deadman's Bay and Kent's Godwin Sands. The decade in which disasters peaked seems to bave been the 1880s, though there would be a continuing mix of miracles and disaster in the twentieth century.

The Great Western Railway's steamer *South of Ireland* terminated her Christmas Day cruise in 1883 on the rocks on the edge of Worbarrow Bay. Appropriately for the date all aboard were saved. The rocks had completely holed the vessel and she became a total wreck.

The *Palata*, a 1,408-ton steamer, was wrecked on the Kimmeridge Ledges on 15 May 1886 though all the passengers and crew were also rescued on that occasion. To the west of Kimmeridge Bay, the projecting shelf of Broad Bench claimed the schooner *Liberty* on 25-26 September 1868, and the smack *Ceres* on 21 March 1886. The brigantine *Wild Wave* was a total loss on Peveril Ledge on 23 January 1875. Another brigantine, *Commodore*, was a total wreck on Encombe Ledge on 18 August 1877.

Sometimes the sea released its catch, as with the schooner *Minnie* which was hard on Kimmeridge Ledges on 11 January 1890 but rescued by a decent tide. Likewise when the Russian sailors of the 3,512-ton steamer *Cerera* rammed the rocks a mile east of St Alban's Head on the night of 14 April 1907, they were fortunate to be pulled clear.

Smuggling – formerly the principal trade along this coast, though less romantic than it is often portrayed. Something of the ruthless reality comes across in this story recorded by Llewellyn Pridham in *The Dorset Coastline* about a smuggler who was stoned to death at Cow Corner, the western end of Worbarrow beach (SY 860 804): "There is a queer legend about this lonely piece of shore, which only serves to enhance its eeriness. A smuggler took to his heels when beset by the revenue men, and not knowing that the beach ended up against a precipice ran like the wind, followed much slower by the officers of the law who knew that they already possessed him. Turning at bay he was forced to take to the sea, where he was stoned till he died.The story goes on to relate that at the waning of the moon, during the quietude of the night, sounds of strife can still be heard and half choked screams."

Neither side had a monopoly of the violence. For instance, a brief disturbance on a Lulworth cliff that ended with murder rated only the following short paragraph in a local paper of 1832: "An encounter at Lulworth between a Preventive Officer named Knight and his assistant and a party of smugglers resulted in the officer being thrown over the cliffs. He died soon after being found."

The story was told more fully on a gravestone in Weymouth's Bury Street cemetery. There is no longer any Bury Street cemetery. It was cleared of bones in 1974 and replaced, in the fashion of the decade, by a multi-storey car park. Knight's stone has been rehoused in the town's museum:

"SACRED TO THE MEMORY OF LIEUT. EDWARD KNIGHT, RN, OF FOLKESTONE, KENT, AGED 42, WHO IN THE EXECUTION OF HIS DUTY AS CHIEF OFFICER OF THE COASTGUARD WAS WANTONLY ATTACKED BY A BODY OF SMUGGLERS NEAR LULWORTH ON THE NIGHT OF 28TH OF JUNE, 1832, BY WHOM AFTER BEING UNMERCIFULLY BEATEN

HE WAS THROWN OVER THE CLIFF NEAR DURDLE DOOR FROM THE EFFECTS OF WHICH HE DIED THE FOLLOWING DAY. BY HIS UNTIMELY DEATH THE PUBLIC SERVICE HAS LOST A VALUABLE AND UNIVERSALLY RESPECTED OFFICER AND SINCERE FRIEND AND HIS WIFE AND FAMILY AN AFFECTIONATE HUSBAND AND KIND FATHER."

That memorial comes from the closing years of the smugglers' era. Two centuries of heavy taxation on spirits that brought prosperity to those in a position to evade the excise — the fishermen of the South Coast, and those in the manorial homes who financed illicit cargoes, gambling on the fact that four out of five runs came safely through the coastguards' net.

Other accounts survive from the opening period of the history of organised illegal importation of spirits and wines, tobacco, pepper and other taxable luxury items. By 1727, the state's annual income from excise duty had reached nearly £2,500,000. Already the business of evasion was far more successful and sophisticated than the inadequate machinery established to ensure that duties were paid.

Phillip Taylor, Collector of Customs at the port of Weymouth, wrote on 11 April 1719:

"We have from Sunday last searched Lulworth Castle belonging to Mr Weld, a Roman Catholic, and many other suspect houses in East and West Lulworth. In the house of Edward Bagwell, a tennant of Mr Weld, we seized about four gallons of Brandy and about 12 lb. of pepper, from whence we proceeded into the Isle of Purbeck and places adjacent where we seized one anchor of red wine and two anchors of vinegar. And knowing it is the constant practice of smugglers to carry their goods off the coast as soon as possible after landing, as Blackmore [Vale] is the most disaffected part of the county abounding with the greatest number of dangerous rogues, two whereof we hear were

Thursday last committed for declaring themselves for the Pretender, and consequently a place very fit to be searched, we have accordingly narrowly searched several houses and there seized yesterday in the home of Jacob Fox two anchors of Brandy."

A year before, Taylor had written in despair to his superiors:

"The smuggling traders in these parts are grown to such a head that they bidd deffiance to all Law and Government. They come very often in gangs of sixty to one hundred men to the shoar in disguise armed with swords, pistolls, blunderbusses, carbines and quarter staffs; and not only carry off the goods they land in deffiance of the officers, but beat, knock down and abuse whoever they meet in their way; soe that travelling by night neer the coast and the peace of the country are becoming very precarious; and if an effectual Law be not speedily passed, nothing but a military force can support the officers in discharge of their dutyes."

In 1766 the Government increased the scope of smuggling when it banned the importation of foreign made silks and velvets to placate the British weavers. Fifty thousand workers had marched on Westminster a year before to protest that their trade was collapsing under overseas competition. Rioting and attacks on the houses of importers continued into the night and the outcome was a set of restrictions that gave smugglers a new job.

The job of landing the kegs and distributing the goods fell to a wider section of the community who played their part in a national network of secret routes and caches. Most of the Purbeck cargoes were shipped out again, across the waters of Poole Harbour, to avoid risk in leaving by the island's easily guarded land exit. Landings were made on the northern harbour shore at Keysworth, West Holton, Lytchett Bay, Hamworthy and Parkstone. The waggon routes inland lay open from these lonely places.

Some loads, however, did go out through the front door of Purbeck. W.M. Hardy recorded in his *Smuggling Days in Purbeck* a rare occurrence of boldness in daylight: "In the year 1796 my grandfather, then a boy ten years old, and living in Wareham, was an eyewitness to a stroke of astonishing bravado and reckless defiance of the the law in broad daylight. Well did he remember one day seeing two waggons pass through the main street of the town, coming from the direction of Purbeck and going on to Northport. They were loaded with tubs and the devil-may-care smugglers, with great sticks in their brawny hands, were seated on top of them, evidently ready to defend their property should occasion for doing so arise . . ."

Frequent landings were made on the cliffs and bays of southern Purbeck, especially Worbarrow, Brandy Bay (an apposite name), Kimmeridge, Chapman's Pool, Winspit, Dancing Ledge, Tilly Whim, and Durlston Bay. Easier for operations was Studland Bay with its wide sandy bottom and ample areas of dense cover. Often, kegs were hidden temporarily under seaweed that had been dragged up the beach for fertiliser. From there the tubs were carried across the heath to Brand's Point, Greenland or Redhorn Quay and loaded into flat-bottom canoes, used legitimately as platforms for punt-guns, to be rowed to the other side of the harbour. The closely watched entrance to the harbour at Haven had to be avoided.

Six Purbeck smugglers appeared at the Lent assize which opened at Dorchester on 14 March 1834. They were aged between sixteen and thirty-five, and their entry in the *Calendar of Prisoners at Dorchester Prison*, now at Dorset Record Office, reads:

"Committed by the Reverend Nathaniel Bond and the Reverend George Pickard, Junior, charged on the oaths of Lieutenant Henry John Carr, Chief Officer of the Coast Guard stationed at Kimmeridge in the Isle of Purbeck, and others, at a place called Gadcliffe [Gad Cliff, above the appropriately named Brandy Bay] in the parish of Tyneham, in the said Isle of Purbeck on the evening of the 31 January, they being there assembled in order to be aiding and assisting in the illegal landing, running or carrying away, prohibited goods. — Warrant dated 10 February 1834. — *Death recorded.*"

That record is misleading: at the Midsummer sessions on 1 July that year their death sentences were commuted to hard labour for a year in each case. Philip Draper told me in 1969 about a smugglers' hiding hole constructed at the west end of Gad undercliff, near Pondfield Cove, which he had been shown by a Worbarrow fisherman in the 1930s.

The last person who remembered the smugglers of Purbeck was Walter Miller of Chaldon Herring who was born in Rose Cottage on the Burning Cliff at Ringstead, 24 June 1890. He looked back for me, in 1971, to those figures of the past:

"My grandfather, Joseph Miller, was born at Worbarrow. He died at West Lulworth in about 1911, aged about seventy-eight. All the Miller family were smugglers before the Crimean War. The landowners and gentry smiled at this as it wasn't considered a crime. If they were caught with their gear and their boat an all that, they had six months imprisonment, but not hard labour.

"One of my great uncles did his time at Dorchester. He was unlucky to be caught, and when he came out of jail, he was met by the squires and whatever and was taken to the Kings Arms for a good meal; because cellars were getting low, you see. They condoned it in a way.

"We have a grapple, used to grapple up the barrels when they were sunk at the bottom. Grandfather, Joseph, had to give up smuggling in 1854 because the Russian war broke out and all the coastguards were called up to serve in the Baltic fleet. Then they recruited all the smugglers to be extra-men, as they called them: that is, coastguards.

"Old Harry Vye and my grandfather and a few more had to sit on the cliff and watch for the smugglers who didn't come! They couldn't risk doing the two jobs at once. That's George Begg [he pointed to a photograph]. He didn't like me; he used to think I was too mischief-full or something. There was a story of a coastguard who accused a smuggler of doing something, pulled out a revolver and shot this man. What comforted the smugglers was that this coastguard was called up to the fleet in the Russian war, got frostbite – and both his ears fell off. They said it was retribution.

"George Begg was at Ringstead and had a boat of his own and went to Cherbourg to get a load. He had a twenty-two foot *lerret* [Dorset dialect word for a rowing boat pointed at both bow and stern] and built a house at Ringstead to conceal it. The boat wasn't on the beach; when he wanted to he just had to slip it out and go to France. He was a clever old fellow. He used to wear those white trousers when I was a boy: I suppose he died about eighty-five in 1898. Dr Good from Dorchester came twice and said he was finished, but George Begg got up and went to sea again. He had another bout and this time the doctor said: 'I think he will do.' He died! Dr Good was wrong in all his predictions. It didn't enhance my father's opinion of doctors. 'No bloody good,' he used to say. Good for nothing, that lot were."

Miller mentioned the Vye family. They had a reputation, indeed a record, for being smugglers. Three members of the same Lulworth Cove household each spent six months in prison between 1839 and 1844 – namely John Vye (aged 40), Henry Vye (aged 22), and Charles Vye (aged 19).

Smythe/Weld/Fitzherbert – desirable **Maria Anne Smythe** [1756-1837] was described by diarist Elizabeth Pearce as "more beautiful and gracious than almost any living woman". In 1775 she married Edward Weld of

Lulworth Castle but he died the same year. It had been his second marriage. Her second marriage, in 1778, was to Thomas Fitzherbert, but he died in 1781. Her third serious relationship is that for which she is remembered.

In 1785 Mrs Fitzherbert met and married the Prince of Wales, later George IV, but the ceremony was without the consent of George III, and therefore invalid by the Marriage Act of 1772. The Prince was aware of his constitutional problem but hoped to carry off a fait accompli; instead he was fated to a disastrous second marriage with Caroline of Brunswick.

Of the so-called morganatic wife, Mrs Fitzherbert, Elizabeth Pearce writes in *Old Portland*: "I've heard the turn of her wrist and ankle were such as marked her birth: a high-bred woman's walk and carriage is as noted as a thorough-bred horse's; and that her countenance was wonderful out of the common. Young, and rich, and beautiful! A wife, as all believe; though still no wife in the eyes of the world. To think the son of our King should so shame a gracious lady!"

Her disengagement from the Lulworth estate was riven with ill-feeling. Edward Weld had drafted a new will to give her "everything in his power" but it seems he became too ill to sign it; and at any event much of his property was held in trust. The most distressing detail for Maria was that the family claimed the pearls which she insisted Edward had given her.

They finally agreed that she could keep them for life and on her death in 1837 they were returned to Lulworth. It is only to be expected for a landed family to dispute a will, but they can hardly have seriously believed that Edward had merely loaned Maria her jewellery.

South of Ireland – steamer operated by the Great Western Railway, wrecked on rocks in Worbarrow Bay [25 December 1883].

Squirrel Cottage mounds – an inexplicable set of small circular mounds lie in woodland south-west of Squirrel Cottage at East Holme (SY 905 852), on the boundary of Lulworth Ranges between flags nos. 41 and 42.

They now number about fifty but more than twice that number were noted in 1860.

J.H. Austen described them and observed that trees planted on them "were of much larger size than those upon level ground". He dug into many of them and found burned furze. Two were excavated in the 1960s and Professor Dimbleby of the Commonwealth Forestry Institute examined pollen samples. The mounds contained raw humus buried "not later than mediaeval times and not earlier than the Iron Age."

Nothing was found to indicate their date and the only other relevant fact is that one appears to overlap the edge of a Bronze Age round barrow. Two other barrows lie on the gravel knoll.

Stair Hole – the principal setting for the West Lulworth geology lesson (SY 822 798). The bowl-shaped depression above the rocks can act as a sound-box and at any time of the year you are liable to hear a teacher shouting its meaning at his impatient herd. Basically it goes like this: Lulworth is the best example in Britain of different rates of coastal erosion. To the west is a magnificent sea-arch at Durdle Door.

At Stair Hole there is a gash and another sea-arch where the waves are breaking through the limestone to gouge out a mini-Lulworth Cove. The rocks display tilted and twisted strata where movement of the harder Portland stone rucked up the Middle and Upper Purbeck beds. Geologists call it the "Lulworth Crumple".

To the east the sea has made a proper breakthrough and created Lulworth Cove. These are classic landforms.

Steeple – little village but big parish, of 3,364 acres, partly inside and then eastward of the Lulworth Ranges. Includes the country house estate of Creech Grange and the nearby hamlet of Creech. Its former western hamlet of West Creech and farmstead at Lutton are now both inside the Lulworth Ranges [since 1943].

The parish extends from the sea, at Kimmeridge Oil Well, inland to the chalk ridge of the Purbeck Hills and then down on the north side to Grange Heath and Hurst Mill. This was of some age and had one Henry Hurst as a seventeenth century miller [1636]. There was and is nothing but heathland for a mile, in all directions, but all this area lies inside the no-go area of the Royal Armoured Corps' Heath Range.

Steeple Manor House – the attractive country house 150 yards north of Steeple church (SY 912 810) was built about 1600. Its hall survives from this period but the frontage and wings are from its enlargement by Roger and Ruth Clavell [1698-1703].

Steeple parish church – dedicated to St Michael, in the centre of this little cul-de-sac village (SY 912 809). Basically it is a twelfth century nave with a sixteenth century tower added at the west end, and a Victorian chancel replacing the original one, plus two side chapels.

The north transept was added by Edward Lawrence [1616] and has his initials, plus arms that incorporate those of the Washington family who were to produce the first President of the United States of America.

The Bond family of Blackmanston, half a mile south-east, built the tiny sixteenth century south chapel, off the chancel. Their grand old man, William Bond [died 1636], who "lived at Blackmanston eighty-two years", to quote John Hutchins, was amongst the first to be buried there.

Then the Bond family came to Creech Grange [1685] and their subsequent memorials reflect their rising fortunes and tenure that would last for centuries.

The barrel organ was made by W. Walker and Co of London [circa 1860] and the American organ [1872] is from the church at Tyneham, having been removed when the village was occupied by the Army [1943].

Steeple Stars and Stripes – the coat of arms on a stone shield in the porch of Steeple church is identical with that on the signet ring of George Washington [1732-99], the first President of the United States. The same design also appears four times on the roof inside, and on the north wall of Affpuddle chancel.

The stars and stripes (bars and mullets, technically) of the Washington family joined the crusader cross of the Lawrences with the marriage of Edmund Lawrence and Agnes de Wessington [1390].

Creech Grange, immediately east of the Lulworth Ranges (SY 912 823), became the family's Dorset seat and their tombs are below the aisle of its parish church in Steeple village.

Stickland – lifeboat coxswain **William Stickland** [1818-81] of Stickland's Cottage, South Egliston, Tyneham (SY 899 791) was the hero of many rescues. Kimmeridge Lifeboat Station [opened 1868] was only 300 yards south-east of his home. Its 28-foot, five-oared boat was the *Mary Heape*.

During a gale on 8 December 1872 she rescued fifteen men, the crew of the Norwegian ship *Stralsund*, from the Kimmeridge Ledges. Stickland, a fisherman, was given the principal credit for that rescue and would save many more lives before he retired. He was buried in Tyneham churchyard in March 1881 on his death at the age of sixty-four.

Stralsund – Norwegian ship wrecked on the notorious Kimmeridge Ledges, with her crew of fifteen being plucked to safety by William Stickland and the Kimmeridge Lifeboat [8 December 1872]. It was the spectacular rescue of this short-lived station, amply justifying its existence, but shortage of manpower caused its closure [1896].

Thorn Barrow – a large Bronze Age burial mound, ten feet high, which was overgrown by heathland vegetation at Povington (SY 878 819), north of the Purbeck Hills in the parish of Tyneham, until it was accidentally destroyed by the military in 1971. There are three other adjacent round barrows in this part of the Lulworth Ranges.

Three Lords' Barrow – this Bronze Age burial place is just a low mound placed on a heathland knoll in western Purbeck but it serves as the meeting point of four parishes – East Holme, Arne, Church Knowle and Steeple (SY 915 847). It is also now on the boundary of the Lulworth Ranges, beside red flag no. 43.

A piece of old church window has been planted in the top of the three foot high mound as a boundary stone. It probably came from the old priory church at East Holme which was an outlying cell of Cluniac monks from Montacute Abbey, Somerset. The building at East Holme was pulled down in 1746.

Turbeville – estateless **John Turbeville** [died 1703], of the family whose demise inspired one of Thomas Hardy's most famous novels, hoped for "a better inheritance" in the next life. His inscription in a small field called Canary Close, near the Vicarage at East Lulworth, recorded the demise of a member of the Turbeville family who had asked to be buried "near a little ash tree about the middle of the west hedge". It was Hardyesque in its wording, being redolent of the faded family fortunes that inspired Hardy's *Tess of the d'Urbervilles*.

The stone hinted at a lost inheritance: "In Memory of John Turbeville, gent, who died in the ninth day of August, 1703, in assured hope, by the merits of Jesus Christ to receive a better inheritance. Also for Mary his wife who died in 1716." The estate listed in his will comprised the land known as Canary, "the forsear of two acres of Hay Ground lying in West Holme Meadow", and whatever farm stock the land supported.

Tyneham – the special South Coast time-warp, inside the Lulworth Ranges. Had it not gone under military occupation six days before Christmas in 1943, and then failed to return to peacetime life as had been pledged, I doubt if it would now be hallowed as a place of such sacred memory. Other coastal valleys in western Purbeck, such as Lulworth and Kimmeridge, have their own charms and nostalgia of the sort that Women's Institutes are so good at gathering.

Tyneham post-1945 could have been much the same; nice, yes, but hardly unique. What brings it the accolade is that it alone has since returned to something approaching the unkempt wilderness of a mediaeval landscape at the fringes of civilisation. The clearance of population from the entire 3,003 acre parish was at the order of Churchill's War Cabinet, for the benefit of the Gunnery Wing of the Royal Armoured Corps Fighting Vehicles School at Lulworth Camp.

They were to train the American and British tank crews who were destined to open the Second Front against the Nazis in Normandy. Co-beneficiaries of the military's good fortune in being allowed to retain their war-gains have been the animals, the wild roe deer, and the birds; everywhere there are birds. Military ecology, paradoxically, can win the green vote. It is well ahead of the county's normal countryside, the land that has since gone through the Agricultural Revolution of ploughing and chemicals, both in the numbers and diversity of its wildlife species across both flora and fauna.

That is why there are always buzzards circling overhead and why the peregrine falcon came back from near man-inflicted extinction to breed in the Lulworth Ranges ahead of its reappearance in civilian countryside. Other deft swing-wing birds of prey such as the merlin and the hobby never stopped breeding in army lands as their like ceased to be seen in most of lowland England.

Tyneham and the ruins of its scattered farms and cottages have been engulfed in a jungle that is still largely a forbidden land despite the network of permissive weekend and summer holiday paths, the Lulworth Range Walks, that are opened when tank firing is suspended. Most of the parish remains far from these paths. Explosions are taken by nature in its stride, as much a part of the way of the world as thunder and lightning, with bird-song beside the trenches being a phenomenon found in the war-poets of Flanders and the Somme.

The other Tyneham paradox is that life there has been remembered with a clarity undiminished by the passing of decades. The minds of those who lived there prior to 1943 remain uncluttered by subsequent events. They are recalled in a soft half-focus that suits the image of a rural idyll. It was a piece of feudal Dorset, still in the fiefdom of the Bond family who had owned its valley for generations, though that was always recounted as a strength rather than anything questionable.

Not that Dorset readily accepted that one of its most cherished coastal valleys would be yielded into perpetual military occupation.

Post-war opposition to the retention of the Purbeck Tank Gunnery Ranges by the War Office stretched across the political spectrum and was at an intensity that makes modern local affairs sound quite tame. South Dorset's Member of Parliament was Viscount Hinchingbrooke,

Conservative, who had served in France in 1940 and afterwards on the General Staff of Home Forces. He made an uncompromising speech to the Society of Dorset Men gathered at their annual dinner in London's Connaught Rooms on 5 May 1947:

"The part of Dorset I love best, extending from Corfe to Lulworth, is bound like Andromeda to the rock. The War Office dragon is breathing its fire and smoke over her, and we, like Perseus, must go to her rescue.

"There were two occasions in history when the sons of Dorset rose in defence of her coasts. At the time of Napoleonic menace, so wonderfully depicted by Thomas Hardy in *The Dynasts*, every man leapt to his allotted post in order to defend her shores, and again in September 1940, when the alarm was once more given. In both cases the alarm was unfounded. But we must not allow it to be said that Dorset men only move to action when the alarm is false.

"Today there is an urgent alarm — South Dorset is gradually being turned, by an insidious process, into a military encampment — and the project will be backed up by all the mercenary and commercial forces which come in its train. We must attempt some concrete action to prevent this going any further. We should make it the objective of this dinner, and indeed of county activities as a whole, to release our county as far as possible from military control.

"What is the use of a great standing army and fleets of aircraft if the source and inspiration of patriotism is lacking through the spoliation of our countryside?"

Hitchingbrooke, however, was to be no stranger to lost causes. In 1962 he succeeded his father as the tenth Earl of Sandwich but disclaimed the peerage for life in an attempt, which failed, to remain in the House of Commons. As president of the Anti-Common Market League he led the resistance to Britain joining the European Economic Community. It was as Victor Montagu that he retired to

Mapperton Manor in the hills of west Dorset between Beaminster and Powerstock.

Tyneham was emotive in 1947 and indeed can be today. Margaret Bond wrote to me on 8 February 1987 from Culliford House in Dorchester where she was about to celebrate her 95th birthday. She was the third daughter of William Bond who had owned Tyneham from 1898 until his death in 1935. Her memories, therefore, were quite unique. "Like so many other things one did not bother to think of whys and wherefores until all the older generations have gone. Now I am the last of my generation of Tyneham and Grange Bonds."

She lived in Tyneham House until the war made its first demands in about 1941 when the Royal Air Force erected a coastal radar station on the ridge east of Tyneham Cap. The Bonds went to live in the next house on the estate, the Gardener's Cottage, between Tyneham House and Tyneham Farm.

Margaret Bond was brought up to believe that as landowners her family had duties and obligations as well as rights. Her father had made the Ocean Seat, high on the side of Tyneham Cap and with a superb view of the Channel shipping: "The original one was exactly in the position you describe. It was where the footpath which ran all along the top of Gad Cliff from Worbarrow left the hilltop and went winding round the lower part of Tyneham Cap to descend to South Tyneham and South Egliston.

"When my father succeeded his uncle in 1898 there was a seat already in place. We thought it was for the uncle's two sisters who used to be taken up there in a carriage, all through the Great Wood. Ladies in those days did not possess walking out shoes! Some time after we went to live there, my father had a really superior shelter built of Purbeck stone, high enough at the back and sides to keep off wind and on the open side, a flat-topped stone wall the right height to sit on comfortably if the wooden seat was full up."

The family sent one of its sons to South Africa in 1899 for the Boer War:

"When my eldest brother returned from South Africa after a terrible time shut up in Ladysmith very badly wounded, my parents decided to give the church an organ as a thanksgiving. Before that there was only a harmonium.

"Then came the question of heating, damp being very bad for the organ. I suppose there was no kind of heating at all, though one old resident told me she believed some people brought to church with them small oil lamps to stand at the side of their pew.

"A hideous but efficient black iron 'tortoise' stove, with a black iron pipe all up the wall and out through the roof, was put in; it stood in the corner on the left-hand side between the nave and the chancel."

In 1911, beside the village water tap at the steps to the churchyard, Margaret Bond planted the oak which replaced an old and dangerous elm tree which her father had felled.

I had mentioned one of the villagers who was old then: "The reference to dear Louis Stickland brings back memories of him even though he died as long ago as the 1914-18 war. He and his son, Will, though fishermen by trade, were also very clever craftsmen. As well as building boats in their large boathouse at Charnel, on the west side of Kimmeridge Bay, they were expert builders in stone.

"In 1900 my father wanted to have a shed in the Lower Horseclose, near Shoemaker's Lane, as there was no shelter for young cattle in that part of the straggling farm. Louis and his son not only built the very substantial open-fronted shed but they opened a quarry near the top of Shoemaker's Lane to provide that material.

"When I remember Louis he was a regular attender at morning service in Tyneham church. Though much nearer

Kimmeridge where he lived — his one-storey house was at the lower end of South Egliston Gwyle — it was in Tyneham parish. On Sundays he always dressed in a black frock coat and wore a strange kind of black top hat. He chose the hard way to reach Tyneham, by coming up the gwyle and then climbing the quite stiff side of Tyneham Cap to the Ocean Seat to slope down outside the Great Wood to pass Tyneham Farm. Going home he always took the easier way, up the road and along the top of the Knap to Shoemaker's Lane and so over the hill to Egliston again.

"We never knew why he always came the hard way."

Similar recollections have come to me from a collection of Tyneham ex-residents, descendants and admirers who are now dispersed across Britain and the globe. The latest batch recall Worbarrow fishermen such as Jack Miller at Sea Cottage and Tom Miller and his father, Henry Miller, in Hill Cottage. A cottage in the valley there was the home of Beattie and Winnie Mintern. Their smallholding supplied the valley with milk, butter and eggs. The butter-making was carried on in a thatched room at the end of the house. On the opposite side of the stream stood Rose Cottage and the last person to live there was Arthur Stockley and his family. Nearby, in Fern Hollow, lived Charles and Harriette Miller. Reggie Ware, a soldier of the Great War, lived in the range of cottages that are now reduced to a few walls on the right of the track into Worbarrow from Tyneham Gwyle.

A particular gem of a location, tucked immediately beneath the Purbeck Hills on the Flower's Barrow hill-fort side of Baltington Farm, has a name to match. It is one of those placenames that are so evocative of the Dorset up-along and down-along countryside but which the Ordnance Survey balked at recording because they sound so rustic. "Up Under Barrow" was the local name for this cottage — it sums up a different world that we have lost.

North of the chalk spine of the Purbeck ridge is one of the last great expanses of Dorset's Great Heath, on the sand and clays of the Bagshot beds, formerly with a mile-long hamlet of cob, stone and thatch cottages strung along a lane that meandered between the hills and the heath at Povington. That old road, from East Lulworth to West Creech, is now permanently closed.

There is no public access across any part of the tank-firing Heath Range except for the main B3070, from East Lulworth to Holme Bridge. On and south of the Purbeck Hills, however, Tyneham is well covered by the network of Lulworth Range Walks. Generally these are open at weekends, public holidays, and through the month of August.

Multiple entries are given here for places within Tyneham parish but any attempt to visit them on the ground must be made with great care, and obedience to military restrictions and signs, because live ammunition is, or has been, used in quantity across all parts of the area. That applies even to the immediate surroundings of the public access parts of Tyneham Village, where just the other side of the Army fence there are known to be patches of ground where Second World War mortars and other devices lie only inches apart, just under the grass.

Tyneham Cap — 520-feet rounded green summit south-west of the village, rising above the coastal cliffs with a superb view from Portland to St Alban's Head (SY 891 797). Crossed by the coast path of the Lulworth Range Walks.

Tyneham church — the delightful cross-shaped St Mary's parish church, with a bellcote just off centre but no tower, is to the original mediaeval cruciform plan, now inside the Lulworth Ranges (SY 881 806).

Thirteenth century walls survive in the north transept, including external buttresses at the outer corners, and the north side of the nave. Contemporary features include a double-lancet window and a roughly carved double-arched piscina.

Beside the piscina there would have been the altar for what was initially the chantry chapel for the Russel family of the mediaeval Tyneham House. The earliest monument to a valley-owning family is that for John Williams [died 1627] and wife Jane [1636], erected by grandson John Williams in 1641.

A later landowning family's faithful servant has a black marble tablet in an elaborate surround: "Near this place lye ye Body of Elizabeth Tarrant Servant to Mrs Bond of Tineham which station she continued 34 years. To ye Memory of her Prudence Honefty & Induftry, this Monument is erected. She died Auguft ye 2nd 1769 in ye 54 Year of her Age."

The wooden wall panel with the text of verse nine of the 96th psalm is also from the eighteenth century. The rebuilt south transept, with its stone panel above the doorway in the east wall carved with the arms of the Bond family, dates from the time of Rev William Bond who was rector from 1795 until his death, at the age of ninety-five, in 1852. The fourteenth century south porch, tucked away in a corner, was taken down and rebuilt at the west end of the nave, in a sympathetic restoration that preserves its charm. The Royal Commission on Historical Monuments gives the credit "for at least part of this work" to Christchurch architect Benjamin Ferrey.

Writing in 1970, the Commission go on to say that "the chancel is modern". Turning to church historian Fred Pitfield, one finds it is the 1872 work of architect George Crickmay of Weymouth and builder John Wellspring of Dorchester. More modern still was the "handsome new organ" of 1902 which Mr and Mrs W.H. Bond presented as a thank-offering for the recovery of their son, Lieutenant

Bond, from a serious wound received during the siege of Ladysmith.

With the inclusion of the church in the Lulworth Ranges [1943], though it remained the property of the Church Commissioners, perishable contents were dispersed. The organ went to Steeple. The pulpit, which has seventeenth century side panels, was taken to Lulworth Camp chapel. The church plate, notably a cup and cover-paten by Lawrence Stratford of Dorchester [1574] went to Kimmeridge. The building itself was maintained, after a fashion, and survived the years of neglect to become a local museum, though it is accessible only when the Lulworth Range Walks are open.

Tyneham House – surviving back parts of this once magnificent mansion, at the heart of Tyneham valley and now inaccessible in the Lulworth Ranges (SY 888 802), incorporate a fourteenth century hall. Built by the Russel family, it has great oak beams and elaborate timber trusses supporting the roof of stone slates. Henry Williams added a great open fireplace in the eastern room in 1567.

The house was greatly expanded with the addition of its Elizabethan main section, in Purbeck stone, which gave it the status, according to Thomas Bond, of ranking "far before any other ancient mansion now remaining in the Isle of Purbeck" [1867]. He was less enthusiastic that his contemporaries had disfigured the building by inserting high sash windows along the ground floor frontage.

This looked out across lawns edged with palms and other sub-tropical plants that accepted the mild, moist microclimate of the valley. Beyond was an avenue of tall beech trees and above the line of the Purbeck Hills to the north and the inland slopes of Gad Cliff and Tyneham Cap to the south.

Tyneham House was requisitioned in the Second World War for use in connection with a clifftop coastal radar station [1941]. Its apparatus was above Brandy Bay. The rest of the parish came into War Department hands with the extension of the Lulworth Ranges [1943] for the training of American Sherman tank crews in the run-up to D-Day. Post-war retention of the firing ranges led to carved wall panelling being taken from the house to Dorset County Museum, Dorchester, and the Elizabethan main section being reduced to a ruin in the name of conservation [1968], so that its porch and other architectural features could be removed to the country houses of Athelhampton and Bingham's Melcombe.

Tyneham House original porch — the former lawnside single-storey Elizabethan East Porch [dated 1583] was removed from Tyneham House, inside the Lulworth Ranges [1967] and rebuilt at Bingham's Melcombe, Melcombe Horsey (ST 772 022), the residence of the third Baron Southborough, retired boss of Shell Oil. It may have "found a good home", as Alec Clifton-Taylor writes, but it "lost a gable" in the move.

Tyneham House north porch — added to the Elizabethan wing by the Victorians [1861]. Its frontage was removed from Tyneham when most of the building was demolished [1967]. Parts at least, plus other architectural features, were re-erected in the garden of Athelhampton Hall (SY 770 943), then the home of Sir Robert ("Robin") Cooke.

Tyneham oak and fountain — beside the south-east corner of the churchyard wall, the tree was planted by Margaret Bond in 1911, for the coronation of King George V.

Beneath it, recessed in stone, the village tap and trough would soon be dry. Not that the Biblical inscription, from John's Gospel, chapter 4, verses 13 and 14, looked upon water as merely a temporal convenience: "WHOSOEVER DRINKETH OF THIS WATER SHALL THIRST AGAIN: BUT WHOSOEVER DRINKETH OF THE WATER THAT I SHALL GIVE HIM SHALL NEVER THIRST; OUT OF

THE WATER THAT I SHALL GIVE HIM SHALL BE IN HIM A WELL OF WATER SPRINGING UP INTO EVERLASTING LIFE".

Tyneham phone box — splendidly restored and one of the earliest and rarest in the country, being a white concrete K1 Mark 236 affair that pre-dates Sir Giles Gilbert-Scott's famous cast-iron K6 model.

Tyneham's box stands outside the Post Office and was erected by Wilson Coombes in the winter of 1929. He told me that he faced a tirade of abuse from the rector who resented the innovation.

Landowner William H. Bond signed the forms authorising its installation on 29 September 1929. Michael Thomas tells me that this ties in with its wrought-iron roof decoration: "It is a K1 Mark 236. They came into production in 1927, just after the K2, but are more like the K1 Mark 235 which came on stream in 1924. Approximately 4,500 of the K1 Mark 236s were erected, but the ornate roof sign was a later addition, circa 1929."

It would have long ago been replaced by a standard red metal box had peace returned to the valley. Instead it is a focal point for the museum-look village (SY 882 803), though it must be emphasised that it is not in working order — even with shillings and pence.

Tyneham pre-war - at the declaration of hostilities, in 1939, it was an ordinary little community, exceptional only in that it did not have a public house. There had been none in the village itself though Thomas Spencer was recalled as a "beer retailer" in the fishermen's hamlet of Worbarrow for the third quarter of the nineteenth century, when John Lidderdale was master of the Coast Guard Station.

In those days, Worbarrow also had the only local shop, which was run by Joseph Miller. Indeed, when the lobster trade was flourishing, Worbarrow generated most of the area's activity.

By the 1880s, however, the village started to assert itself, with Mrs Ann Mores as shopkeeper in what became the Post Office. Harry Barnes ran it during the Great War. Mrs Edith Herd was postmistress in the 1930s.

On the outbreak of war, Sunday 3 September 1939, Mrs Gwendoline Driscoll was the shopkeeper at the Post Office (telephone Kimmeridge 211). Rev. Humphrey Churchill Money was at the Rectory (telephone Kimmeridge 219), having taken over from Rev Edwin George Clifford Frend in 1937.

Rev Edward Clifford Hawkes, inducted in 1914, seems to have been the rector who objected to Wilson Coombes installing the telephone box outside the Post Office.

At Tyneham House, owner in residence was (William) Ralph Garneys Bond JP (telephone Kimmeridge 223), who inherited the estate on the death of his father, William Henry Bond JP.

Walter Case Smith was at Tyneham Farm, where he had been since 1912. "Leatherjacket" was his nickname. "A cantankerous old sod," a nephew told me. Albert Longman was farming Baltington, as he had also for several decades.

Herbert John House was the farmer at North Egliston. Albert Ernest Cranton was at Lutton Farm, between North Egliston and Steeple, the next village. All concentrated on dairying.

Sarah Minton ran a smallholding at Worbarrow. As for the "private residents" of the directories, listing those with a touch of class, there was Lieutenant-Commander Godfrey E.H. House RN, retired, at South Egliston (telephone Kimmeridge 216) and Miss M. Ellis living in the Bungalow on the cliff-edge at Worbarrow Bay.

This was the line-up of personalities in the coastal valley during the phoney war, before it suddenly became the front-line with the fall of France in May 1940 and the Luftwaffe's instant take-over of the Cherbourg peninsula, only seventy miles south-east. Initially it was a sea war as the Stukas dive-bombed anything that moved between Lyme Bay and the Isle of Wight. They forced the Admiralty to close the Channel to Allied shipping. Then the Germans turned their attention landwards and the Battle of Britain raged through the hot summer of 1940.

Tyneham requisitioned – at the start of the Second World War the red flags of the Lulworth Ranges were just beyond the western edge of this coastal parish. The village was already preparing to do its bit for the war.

There, in 1940, local magistrate Ralph Bond formed the Tyneham Home Guard with himself as platoon commander. He made what he thought would be his major contribution to the war effort in 1941 when the Royal Air Force requisitioned Tyneham House as the support facilities for a coastal radar station that was being set up on the ridge to the east of Tyneham Cap. It was known as RAF Brandy Bay. The Bonds moved into the Gardener's Cottage between Tyneham House and Tyneham Farm. But a further price had to be paid.

The British and American armies, not the Germans, would bring the Second World War into every inch of Tyneham valley on 19 December 1943.

All 3,003 acres of the parish of Tyneham, inhabited by a scattered population of about two hundred and fifty, and other land beneath Dorset's Purbeck Hills were evacuated by direct order from Winston Churchill's War Cabinet. Local councils were not allowed to question the correctness of the decision and censorship prevented any mention in the press of the requisition of the Purbeck training area. Never for one moment were the Tyneham area inhabitants led to believe that their evacuation was other than a temporary measure necessary for winning the war.

All the Tyneham tenants were informed by the War Department land agent that, if they wished, their tenancies would be maintained. The notice served on each of them contained the following words:

"This means that when the War Department has no further use for the property and it is handed back, you have every right to return to the property. It should not be assumed by you that, because the War Department has turned you out, you lose your right of occupying the premises again."

Even though no mention of the Tyneham takeover was permitted in the press, anyone could have sensed the truth from the auction columns of the Dorset County Chronicle on 2 December 1943. Western Purbeck sounded like a disaster zone. Auctioneers Henry Duke and Son offered 313 dairy cows and bulls, nine working horses, 71 sheep, 33 pigs, 167 poultry, four Fordson tractors, and over 700 separate lots of farm implements from the Tyneham valley alone. The farmers were fleeing:

"Tyneham Farm, Tyneham, for Mr S.G. Churchill, quitting.

"Lutton Farm, Steeple, for Mr A.E. Cranton, quitting.

"Baltington Farm, Tyneham, for Mr A.J. Longman, quitting.

"North Egliston Farm, Tyneham, for Mr H.J. House, quitting."

On the other side of the Purbeck Hills there was a similar pattern of tragedy. Thomas Ensor and Son announced dispersal sales at West Creech Farm (for Mr R.C. Cake); Povington Farm (Mr T.W. Wrixon); Searley's Farm, Povington (Arthur Cooper); Jiggiting Corner, Povington (J. Cooper); Weld Arms Farm, East Lulworth (Mrs B. Bonham); The Cat, East Lulworth (Mrs S.P. Damen); Whiteway Farm, East Lulworth (H.J. Sampson); Broadmoor Farm, West Creech (H.C. George); White Hall Farm, West Creech (W. Cake); Rookery Farm, West Creech (Frank Cranton); Hurst Mill Farm, West Creech (A.E. Swain).

There was a sad note at the end of the lists: "The Auctioneers wish to draw special attention to the before mentioned Sales and sincerely trust that all farmers from over a wide area will endeavour to attend as many as possible to assist in the dispersal of the stock on offer, all of which is thoroughly recommended by the Auctioneers."

Frank Cranton was the lucky evacuee as he was able to secure another farm, keep most of his stock, and cancel the "away-going" sale at West Creech. Miss Helen Taylor was evicted from Laundry Cottages, Tyneham, and moved to a council home at Corfe Castle. She preserved the eviction notice which was signed by Major-General Charles Harvey Miller of Southern Command on 16 November 1943 and stated: "The Government appreciate that this is no small sacrifice which you are asked to make, but they are sure you will give this further help towards winning the war with a good heart."

Many of the elderly villagers, like fisherman Jack Miller, of Sea Cottage, Worbarrow, failed to survive their uprooting and died before the war was over.

John Charlton wrote to me from Oxfordshire in 1968 when he saw Jack Miller's Sea Cottage at Worbarrow pictured in ruins in the Dorset County Magazine: "I wonder what has happened to Miggy and her husband with their stuffed cat who used to live in the cottage on the front of your first issue."

The young were able to adapt and make new lives for themselves. Sarah Braisley lived at Egliston in a secluded valley above Kimmeridge Bay. She was the last girl to marry in Tyneham mediaeval parish church, on 23 May 1943. Below this final entry, the marriage register, which spanned nearly 150 years, was stamped twice with a blue oval "Cancelled".

"It was quite a wrench when we moved out. But it was for the good of the country. It was rather exciting in a way for me, but it affected my parents a lot. It meant selling everything."

Poppy Budden, her sister, was then eighteen years old. She emphasised: "We were given an understanding that we would move back there some day. Most people expected to go back. But I don't feel any bitterness about it and I look back on the years at Tyneham as a very happy time."

The reaction of Mrs S.B. White is different: "I find it too painful even to go back and look at Tyneham again. Members of my family are buried in the tiny churchyard and my mother's old homestead on Povington Heath can just boast a pile of stone, part of the chimney stack and a lonely and gruesome looking yew tree."

As the last residents evacuated the valley they pinned a farewell notice on the church door: "Please treat the church and houses with care. We have given up our homes, where many of us have lived for generations, to help win the war to keep men free. We shall return one day and thank you for treating the village kindly."

In December 1947 Clement Attlee's post-war Labour Government admitted in its command White Paper Number 7278:

"In the case of some of the proposed training areas particularly Stamford and the Purbeck tank gunnery school it has been, or may be represented, that pledges were given, or understood to be given, and it will not therefore be necessary to press the point at any public enquiry; at the same time for reasons given in earlier paragraphs, areas for practical training must be provided and it follows that if an area in respect of which a pledge was given were surrendered and a new area taken up, one result would be the eviction of residents in the new area for the benefit of those originally displaced."

That sealed the fate of Tyneham and the heathland hamlet of Povington on the other side of the Purbeck Hills. The Government freely admitted that promises of the land's return "at the end of the emergency" had been given. But Britain's extended firing ranges were part of the

War Office's gains from the Second World War and it was not going to give them away. A public inquiry was duly held in 1948 and the War Minister, John Strachey, upheld “the national interest”.

Tyneham School – display room with an inspiring exhibition of nostalgic images and illustrations of the wildlife of the Lulworth Ranges. The restored building is in the centre of the village, a few yards south-west of the churchyard steps (SY 881 803).

The school closed a decade before the military occupied the parish. It ceased to be a school on 24 March 1932, on the order of the Board of Education, “owing to the small number of pupils and urgent need for economy”.

Tyneham strip fields – plough ridges and about 200 acres of mediaeval cultivation strips, dating from the thirteenth century, survive under the rough pasture of the Lulworth Ranges in Tyneham valley and represent the best preserved collection in Dorset. Contemporary with the village church, the main area extends from the foot of the Purbeck Hills at Whiteway Hill (SY 880 808) in a broad sweep southwards, either side of Rook Grove and then across the whole area between Tyneham village and Tyneham House, and finally upwards on the inland slopes of Gad Cliff to within one field of the edge.

The other great cluster stretches from north-west of North Egliston (SY 897 810) and southwards beside the parish boundary with Steeple all the way to the cliffs at Charnel (SY 902 791). Westwards it spreads beyond South Egliston to lynchets on Tyneham Cap (SY 891 792) and southwards down over most of the gently sloping coastal plain to the hinterland of Broad Bench at Stickland's Cottage (SY 898 792).

There are also several mediaeval hamlets in Tyneham parish which are virtually lost, having shrunken to single farmsteads. An extensive series of such settlement remains is east and south of North Egliston and includes a Chapel Close (SY 895 806). Tyneham village itself formerly covered a much greater area, having cottages and closes across what is now the car-park on both sides of the track between it and Tyneham Farm (SY 883 801). Likewise there was a cluster of habitations south and south-east of Baltington Farm (SY 877 804), including a cross-roads of tracks and another arm that forked to give access on to the western open field.

Tyneham war memorial – marble tablet in Tyneham church, to Henry Balson, Charles Job Cleall, Harry and John Holland, William Meech and Bertram Taylor: "All men must die. It is only given to the few to die for their country."

Vigilant – sailing ship wrecked on the cliffs west of Lulworth [14 December 1825] with the loss of all crew apart from Thomas Parker, the mate. He was saved through the efforts of Coastguard Owen Lloyd who "manifested great alacrity in throwing the rope" which enabled Parker to be "drawn up the high cliff" as the vessel had "almost immediately gone to pieces".

Water Barrows and Ferny Barrows – cluster of Bronze Age burial mounds inside the Lulworth Ranges, south-east of East Lulworth (SY 865 817 to SY 867 816). The two Water Barrows and Ferny Barrows, a bracken-covered pair, lie on the mixed soils between the heath and the chalk ridge of the Purbeck Hills. Their names express the character of the topography. The larger of the Water Barrows is nearly ten feet high and surrounded by a deep-cut ditch that is now twelve feet wide and two feet six inches deep. It is water-filled in winter, and hence the name.

Nearby is Thorny Barrow but this has been virtually eaten by a sandpit.

Barrows with topographical names tend to be prominent mounds in the vicinity of Saxon settlement areas. They therefore tended to be noticed and to be given descriptive names. Numerous other barrows, scattered across the uninviting remoteness of the heath, lack the dignity of a name.

Wealden sands – the basic geology of the valleys of southern Purbeck between the chalk hills and limestone cliffs, seen exposed beside Worbarrow Bay (SY 868 801). Here, from the beach beside the foundations of Sea Cottage, you are treated to bright colours, from red and purple to yellow and white. They are almost up to the standard of the famous Alum Bay sands of the Isle of Wight.

Weld – impotent **Edward Weld** [1705-61] of Lulworth Castle married the Honourable Catherine Elizabeth Aston, Lord Aston's daughter, in an arranged marriage between the two Catholic families. The marriage soon failed and in 1731 husband and wife were in the Arches Court at Canterbury where she had filed a suit for nullity on the grounds of Weld's impotency.

He had undergone treatment for a physical abnormality and was able to successfully defend the case. The secondary issue was of Catherine's libel in bringing the original action and this also went her husband's way.

The nation was able to snigger at the pair in pamphlets on *The Cases of Impotency and Virginity Fully Discuss'd, The whole of the proceedings in the Arches-Court* and *A sequel to the Case*. Eighteen letters between the former couple were published. Catherine went home to Staffordshire, where she died in 1739, which released Edward Weld to marry Teresa Vaughan in 1740 – who redeemed his reputation the following year with the first of five children.

Weld – yachtsman **Joseph Weld** [1777-1863] of Lulworth Castle dominated the Cowes event in the mid nineteenth century. His series of winning vessels included *Alarm, Arrow* and *Lulworth*. He was one of the founders of the Royal Yacht Squadron.

Weld – former landowner **Cardinal Thomas Weld** [1773-1837] of Lulworth Castle had invited French Trappist monks to East Lulworth in 1796. He was then married to Lucy Bridget Clifford. Their only child was Mary Lucy who had been born at Upwey in 1799.

When his wife died, at Clifton in 1815, Thomas reconsidered his life and when his daughter married her second cousin, who became the seventh Baron Clifford, he considered himself free to enter the Roman Catholic ministry.

The family property he renounced in favour of his next brother, Joseph Weld [1777-1863] who became one of the foremost Victorian yachtsmen.

Thomas was ordained priest in 1821 and worked at first in Chelsea and Hammersmith. His rise in the ecclesiastical ranks started as coadjutor to the Bishop of Kingston, followed by his own consecration as Bishop of Amycla, Canada, in 1826.

In 1830 he arrived in Rome and was told a few hours later that Pius VIII was to honour him with the purple, the second Englishman to be admitted to the College of Cardinals since the death of Cardinal Howard in 1694. He lived in the Odescalchi Palace and died in 1837, being buried in the church of S. Maria Aquiro.

The Weld Arms – late eighteenth century thatched inn, probably having always carried this name of the local landowning family as it appears as such in the parish tithe assessment [1841]. Its location (SY 861 821) in the middle of the "new village" of East Lulworth, replacing the old one demolished to put under grass in Lulworth Park [1773-85] indicates it was provided for the benefit of the rehoused populace.

Unexploded Second World War bombs, dropped by the Luftwaffe, would remain wedged in the thatch for half a century before being rediscovered and removed for detonation [1994].

Welfare — the richest and most outrageously treated of all Purbeck shipwrecks, plundered by wreckers in Kimmeridge Bay [1371]. She had been driven ashore whilst sailing up-Channel from her home port of Dartmouth to London.

A special commission was called to try no less than a hundred persons who were implicated in the systematic wrecking of the vessel.

Her difficulties had begun off Portland and were compounded on Kimmeridge beach as those who ran to the news of a wreck found that her freight included thirty-two pieces of cloth of gold, bales of richly embroidered silk, and other merchandise to the value of £2,000 in the currency of that time. That was a huge fortune in the reign of Edward III.

The trial was at Sherborne, at a considerably later date, when many of the accused were found guilty of robbery. Robert Knolles, the owner of the vessel, had been "insulted, wounded and maltreated" and the plunderers had been encouraged and assisted by no less a person than Thomas, Abbot of Cerne Abbas, who had the freight taken and stored in buildings at Kimmeridge. As the owner of the manor of Kimmeridge, the Abbot had a right of wreck to the shore there, but the *Welfare* — because she beached and was held by her crew — was not a "legal" wreck.

Among those convicted when the verdict was reached in 1377 were not only the Abbot and one of his monks, but members of the landed gentry of Purbeck who included William Chaldecote; John Anderbote, of Brinscombe, near Corfe Castle; William Wyat and his son, of Kimmeridge;

John Russel, of Tyneham; John Swanland; and Thomas Gerard, of Corfe Castle.

The right to the wreck of the sea has legally gone with the manor of Kimmeridge and this has not yet been forgotten. Eustace Mansel, of Smedmore, recalled: "In about 1872, I saw a spar washed into Kimmeridge; it was afterwards found to measure three feet thick and seventy feet long. The admiralty claimed it. My father produced a deed of 1554 and it was allowed that it was his right to claim it if not claimed by the rightful owner within a year and a day."

West Lulworth – parish of 2,593 acres and village with plenty of picturesque thatch in its narrow Main Street, with some of the cottages having old pumps and other period artefacts. The parish has Lulworth Cove as its focal point, at the centre of three miles of spectacularly attractive coastline, from Durdle Door to Mupe Bay.

The western third of the parish has been leased by the War Department, now the Ministry of Defence, since 1923, and includes Lulworth Camp (SY 835 805). All the parish is on rolling chalk downland, which extends inland to Belhuish Valley and the former Lulworth Common (SY 827 832).

West Lulworth old church – site of, a hundred yards east of the war memorial on the north side of the Main Road, opposite Spindrift, No. 11 and the Old Bakery (SY 827 807). A plaque records: "THE SITE OF THE OLD PARISH CHURCH, PRE-NORMAN IN FOUNDATION. DEMOLISHED IN 1869 WHEN THE PRESENT CHURCH WAS BUILT."

Certainly it was there in the thirteenth century, and functioned as a chapelry of Winfrith. The former street-side building was roundly condemned at the consecration of its replacement in May 1870, for what had been "its dilapidated condition, and the awkward manner in which the cottages on each side intruded upon its precincts, unpleasantly disturbing the impression of sanctity, solemnity, and dignity that we are wont to accociate with our ideas of a parish church".

Just inside the gate is the grave of Obadiah Legg who died in 1912. To his left is a cross beneath the yew tree to several war heroes, including Charles William Haime, killed at Salonika, and Arthur Edward Silverton RN, commander of HMS *Defence*, who was lost when the armoured cruiser blew up at the Battle of Jutland [31 May 1916]. To the right is a stone to Robert Dudgeon, aged 29, who was the cook aboard the *Avalanche* which sank off Portland after being in collision with the *Forest* in 1877.

West Lulworth parish church — replacing the old church, the present Holy Trinity stands on rising ground at the countryside end of West Road (SY 823 808). It was built in 1869, to designs prepared by Dorchester architect John Hicks who died on 12 February that year, making this a particularly interesting church as Hicks's assistant and work in hand were taken on by George Crickmay's practice in Weymouth.

The junior concerned was Thomas Hardy [1840-1928] who would later make his name as the Wessex novelist and poet.

Wellspring and Son of Dorchester were the builders. Carving of the columns, and a scripture text above a chancel arch, were the work of Benjamin Grassby, also of Dorchester.

Whiteway Hill — Iron Age Celtic field system, on the north-facing slope of the Purbeck Hills, inside the Lulworth Ranges above Povington Heath, Tyneham (SY 876 811). The banks are 60 to 120 feet apart and about a foot high, traceable in places for more than 500 feet, directly up and down the slope in parallel lines. There are also a few cross divisions and the system, on chalk downland, is unbroken across twenty acres.

In terms of contours, the system drops from 607 feet at the top to 270 feet at the foot of the escarpment.

Worbarrow — former fishing hamlet in the south-east corner of Worbarrow Bay, now ruins inside the Lulworth Ranges (SY 872 797). Cottages clustered above around the deeply cut Gwyle stream, in the shadow of conical Worbarrow Tout and a setting that is still breathtakingly picturesque for its natural beauty.

Westward rises the end of the Purbeck Hills, of white chalk cliffs at Flower's Barrow, from a foreground of myriad colours where Wealden sands spread through the spectrum with white, yellow, red, brown and purple hues.

Accessible via the Lulworth Range Walks, the easiest approach being the level one mile along the valley from the car-park at Tyneham village.

Worbarrow Coastguard Station — though previously identified to me as the stone-built house closest to Pondfield Cove at the southern extremity of the hamlet, beneath Gold Down (SY 872 797), I have been corrected by V. Watkinson who lived at Worbarrow until the autumn of 1943: "I notice that you still labour under the misapprehension that Hill Cottage was also the Coastguard Cottage. I'm afraid this is not so. My Gran was born there in 1868. I was told that her father was born there, circa 1835, and I believe that his father was also born there. As you can see, this takes you back to the start of the nineteenth century!

"The Coastguard Station stood between Hill Cottage and the sea (SY 871 797). The Coastguard at Worbarrow were disbanded somewhere around 1910-12. The old squire had the buildings demolished as soon as they left. You can, however, still see some trace of them if you look."

Another correspondent told me of "the great tragedy" that struck the men of Worbarrow Coastguard Station on a Saturday afternoon in March 1865. Five of them set sail to return from Weymouth in a galley laden with stores. They passed a gale warning, displayed from Admiral Fitzroy's signal opposite Weymouth Telegraph Station, forecasting southerly winds. These caught them about three miles from their base, when they were a mile off Lulworth Cove, and a watchman saw the sea strike the galley and sink her "like a stone". There were no survivors.

Worbarrow Minefield — laid along the beach of Worbarrow Bay during the Second World War, when German invasion threatened [July 1940]. Among the last in Dorset to be cleared [1946-47] because it was considered "too dangerous" though in the event it proved to be "a happy minefield" and was free of casualties.

"It gave very little trouble in finalising matters, though a few mines lost to the sea were never accounted for," said officer-in-charge Lieutenant Ralph Ruby [born 1924] who led a combined team of Royal Engineer "sweepers" aided by German prisoners of war.

The usual method of clearance was that mines would be washed out of the ground by a powerful jet of water which was propelled seawards at high pressure. Any mine thus exposed that failed to explode in the process would then be detonated. Application of the technique required considerable expertise and had already claimed the lives of several Sappers on Hampshire beaches.

Worbarrow Tout — inside the Lulworth Ranges, this is the conical sugar-loaf projection, jutting almost as an island into Worbarrow Bay, is the eastern extremity of the Purbeck marble veins (SY 870 795).

It is accessible only when the Lulworth Range Walks are open, a mile from Tyneham car-park, and a stiff climb to the top, which overlooks Pondfield Cove, but most of the geology is under the turf. White gypsum does outcrop in the rock face at the end of the Worbarrow beach, under the near-right face of the Tout, and bits of this make an unusual and almost legitimate souvenir as it is not an endangered specimen.

There is a fossil cycad stump around the tip of the headland but it is inaccessible without climbing ropes and anyway lies beyond the bounds of the army's open beaches.

Pondfield Cove is the small one immediately east of the Tout, still blocked by dragon's teeth anti-tank defences [from 1940]. On the other side the great mile-wide main beach of Worbarrow Bay concealed an extensive minefield, eventually removed by German prisoners-of-war [1946].

Wright — Guardian feature-writer **Patrick Wright** [born 1951], researched the military takeover of Tyneham and subsequent campaigns for its release, in *The Village that Died for England* [1994]. His earlier books were *On Living in an Old Country* [1985] and *A Journey through Ruins* [1991], based on the East End of London.

Though now living in Cambridge he went to school in Dorset, at Bryanston, and has specialised in planning and environment issues. His television productions have also been abrasive, particularly *Brideshead and the Tower Blocks* and *Running down the Mountain* — the latter criticising the making of television programmes, "ensuring that I haven't been asked to do another".

Lulworth Castle: with Roman Catholic Church on one side, and Anglican tower the other